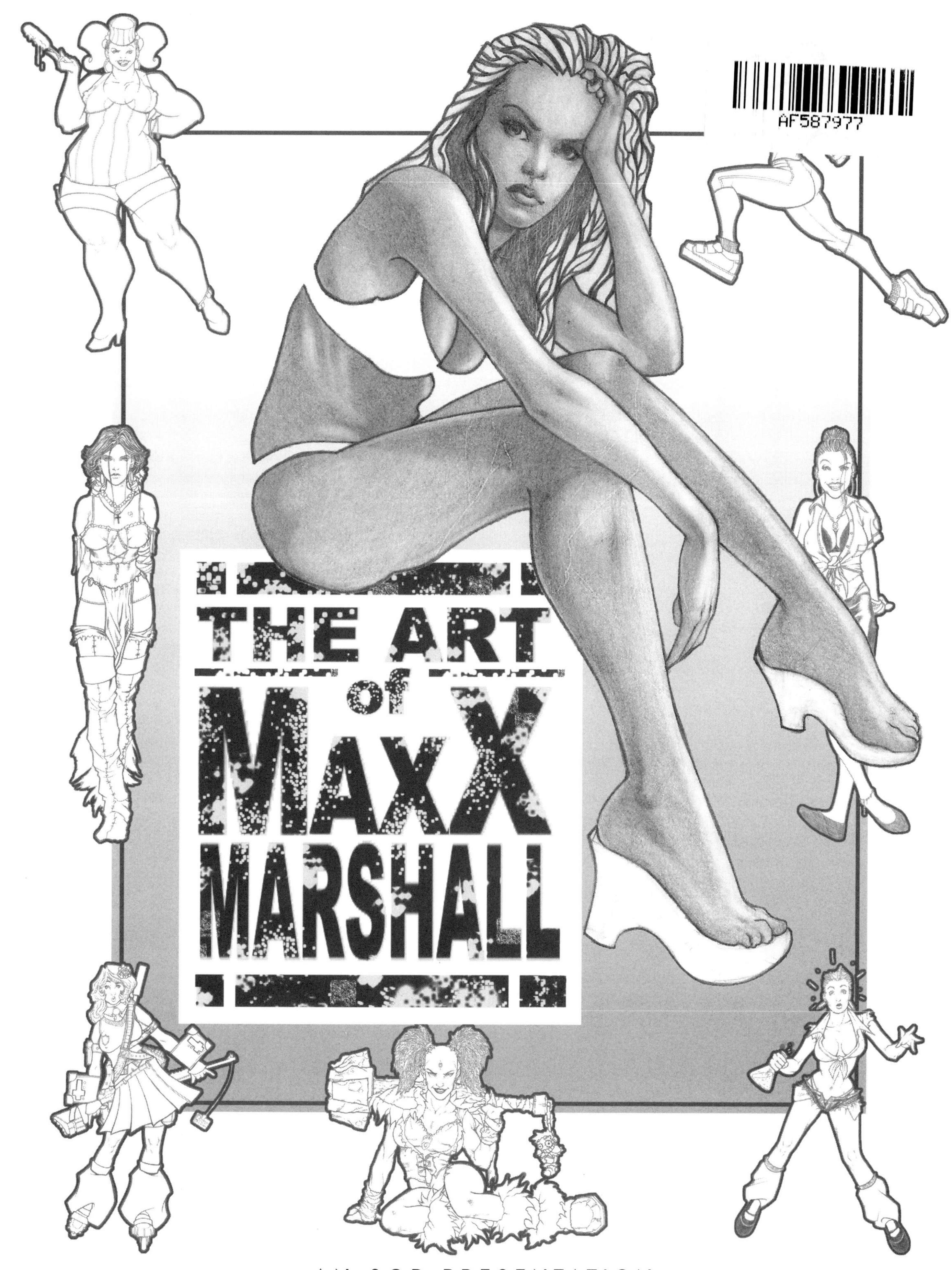

AN SQP PRESENTATION

MASTERING THE MARSHALL ART!

"I LOVE Lines!" Big ones, small ones, thin ones, thick ones and ALL lines in between! "Maxx, can you color that? It'd make the illustration "POP" more!", I hear that all the time. Some times I oblige. I'll paint in some happy colors to get the people off my back for another couple of months. Afterwards, I'll go back to my lines. My beautiful lines.

My love affair with lines started when I was a tyke in Detroit, Michigan. I would sit in church with my mom's pen and draw all over the handouts. I knew that the images in my head weren't the images on the page, and it angered me. If only I could get the lines right, then the little cartoon mouse I was drawing would look like a cartoon mouse instead of an alien dog with pots sticking out of it's head. I stopped drawing after that. I knew that artistic talent was a gift and I knew that I didn't have it. I was good at math and science, and I thought it better to work on a gift that I knew I had. In high school, I started getting the "shakes". No one really knew what it was, but I would get antsy. I would clean, cook, whatever, just to DO something. I decided to start reading. Not the books that teachers TOLD me to read, but stuff off the curriculum. Horror, Adventure, anything I could get my hands on for cheap. I would read these stories and see the imagery in my head. I would dream of nightmarish witches in elevators groping at me and tearing at my clothes. I would wake up and stare at the ceiling unable to return to sleep. One day, I noticed that the images in my head were...cooler/scarier...than the ones I'd seen in books. The giant eyed dragons with bronze-y women fighting them. I wanted eyeless dragons with non cartoon-y claws and jagged teeth that tore and slashed at the knights in beautiful ornate armor. So I sat down and started drawing again, in private, hidden away. Filling sketchbook after sketchbook with mutants, sexy girls, 70's disco gods, heroic alien warriors, you name it, I drew it. Looking back at these books you can see my progression. I started out drawing Saturday Morning Cartoon monsters. I later began drawing Anime Monsters. (O-O-O-O-old school anime monsters) I soon drew comic book monsters, then video game monsters. I drew import Japanese book monsters. Etc. etc. It was then that hard times hit in Detroit. I was out of cash and sleeping at friend's houses. I could draw, but couldn't make a living doing it. I went on my buddy's computer, and pulled up a list of EVERYONE who used artists. EVERYONE!!! I lurked late night at copy shops befriending kids who could get me free copies. I made resumes. Lots of resumes, lots and lots of them. I spent my last remaining cash on the postage to send them out. I received mail by the pound, "Sorry, we don't have a place for you." "Sorry, we don't need anyone.", etc. In all that mail, one letter asked for a call back. I started working for Blizzard Entertainment in California later that month. During that time, I dated long distance for about 5 years. I walked over five miles to work and back ('til I got a bike), was stopped by the police once a week for leaving a "Business Area" at 4AM with a black trench coat. (if you ever meet me, ask me about the time the dispatcher told the officer that he'd stopped me earlier that week.) (well, actually, that's the entire story. So, nevermind). I started drawing for a living. I've since worked for Midway, THQ, Universal, and Sony, designing characters and aliens. I married my long distance girlfriend, got some cats, got a condo, and am most comfortable drawing draped in a GIANT blanket propped up by 2-3 pillows on the floor with a small light. "Maxx, that's not the best place for you to draw, BLAH BLAH BLAH.". Sure, you can say that, but it works for me. It brings me low, and suddenly the world around me is bigger. Couches become buildings, coffee tables become ancient structures. And the cats, giant creatures that can jump up to the tallest points of this world. I sit back, look at all this, look down at the empty page, and let the lines flow.

Sincerely thankful that you bought this book,
-Maxx.

P.S. buy 3 more copies, I need more comics!!!
(JOKING, JOKING...buy 4....)

This book is dedicated to my beautiful wife Dawn.

THE ART OF MAXX MARSHALL
Volume One

Book design by Grassy Knoll Studios.

Published by
SQP Inc.
PO Box 248 - Columbus, NJ 08022

Sal Quartuccio & Bob Keenan - Publishers

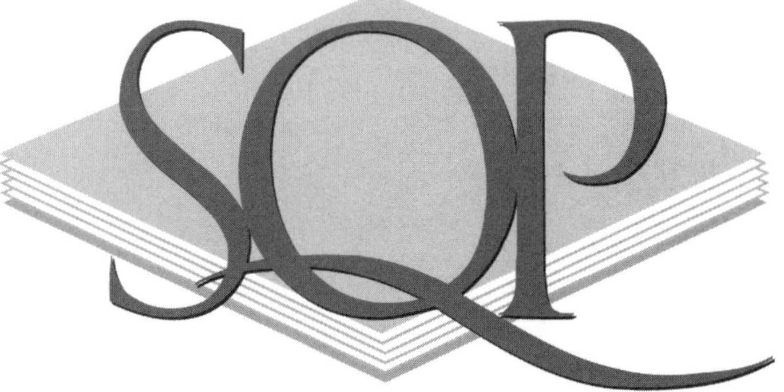

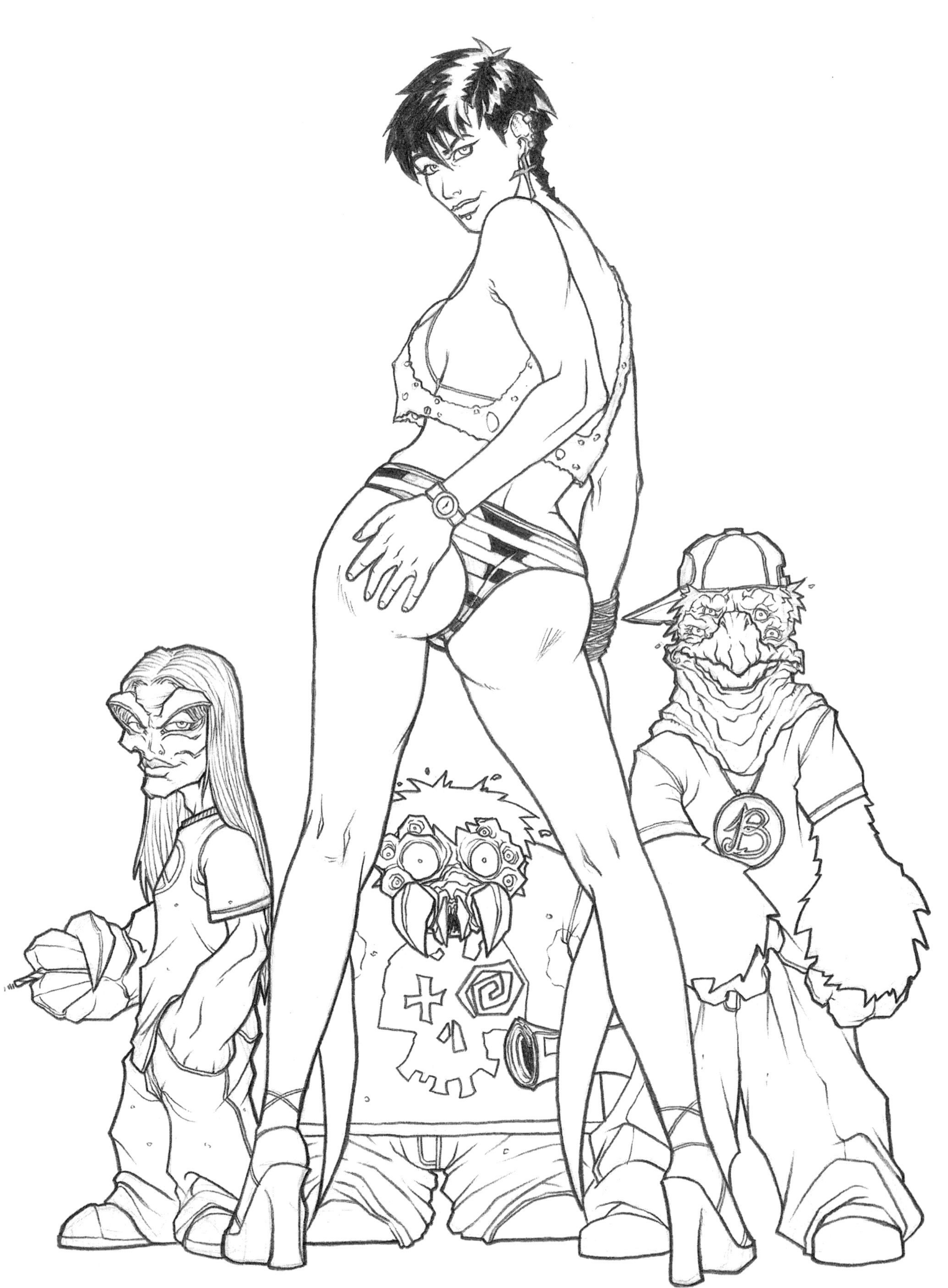

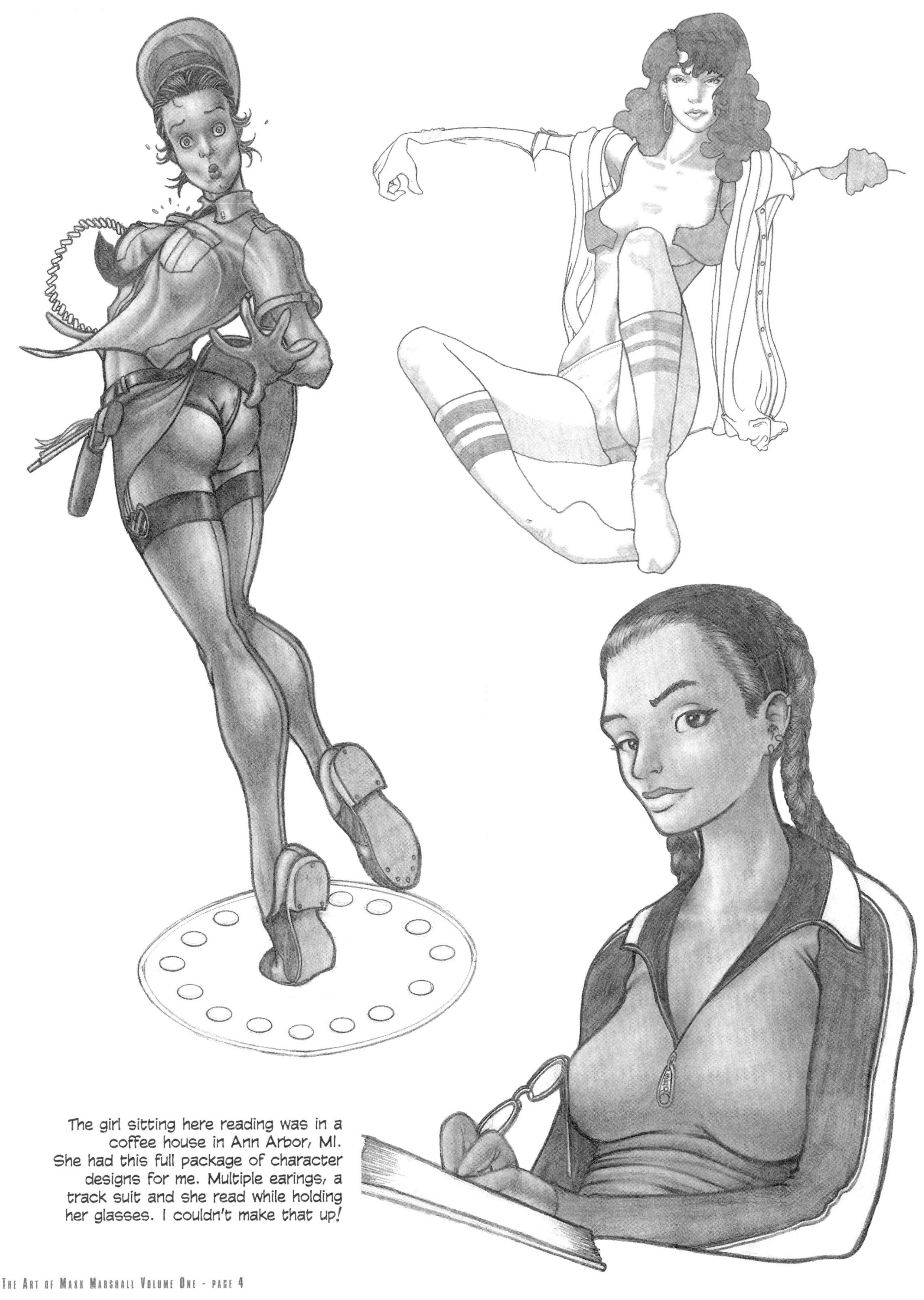

The girl sitting here reading was in a coffee house in Ann Arbor, MI. She had this full package of character designs for me. Multiple earings, a track suit and she read while holding her glasses. I couldn't make that up!

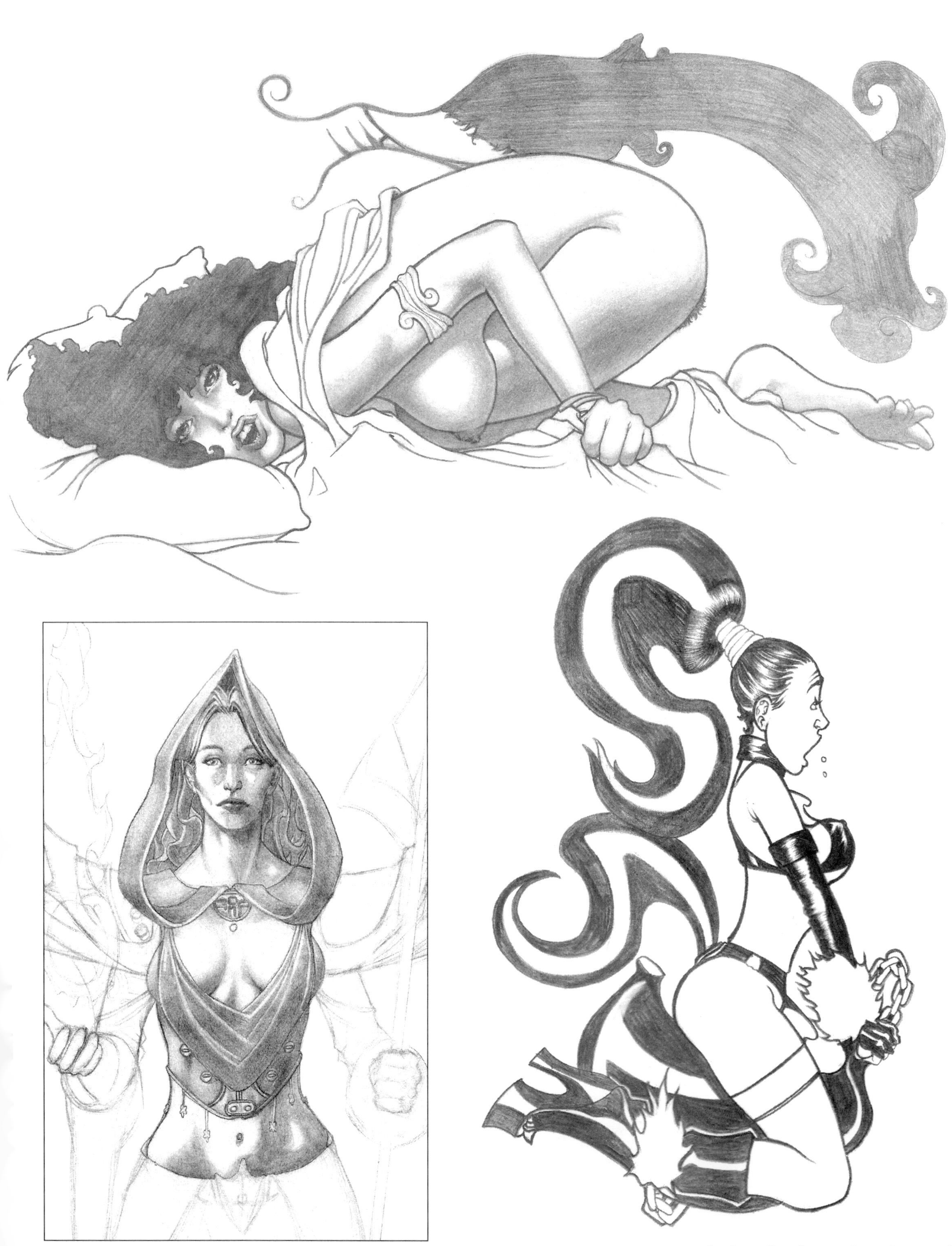

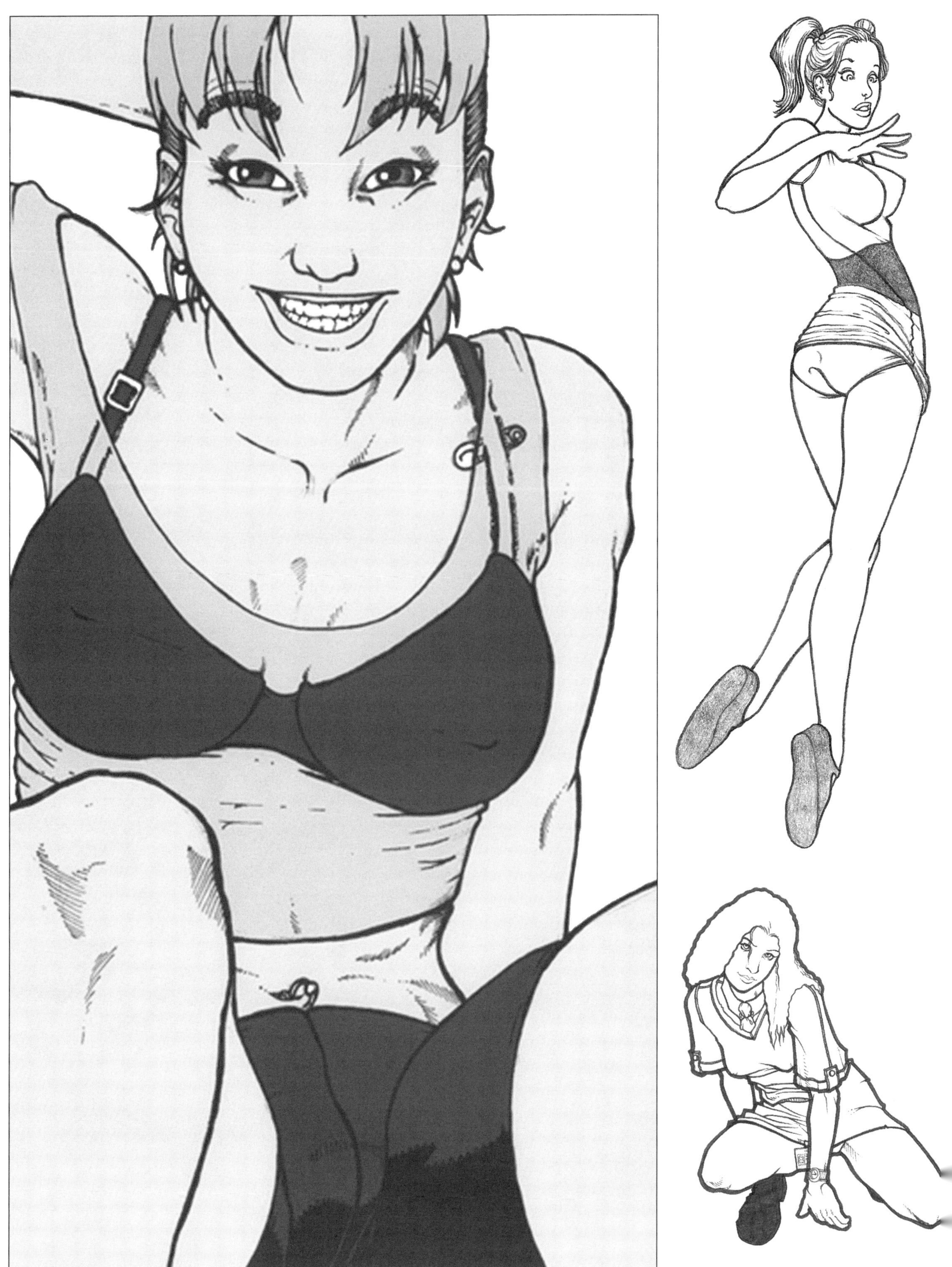

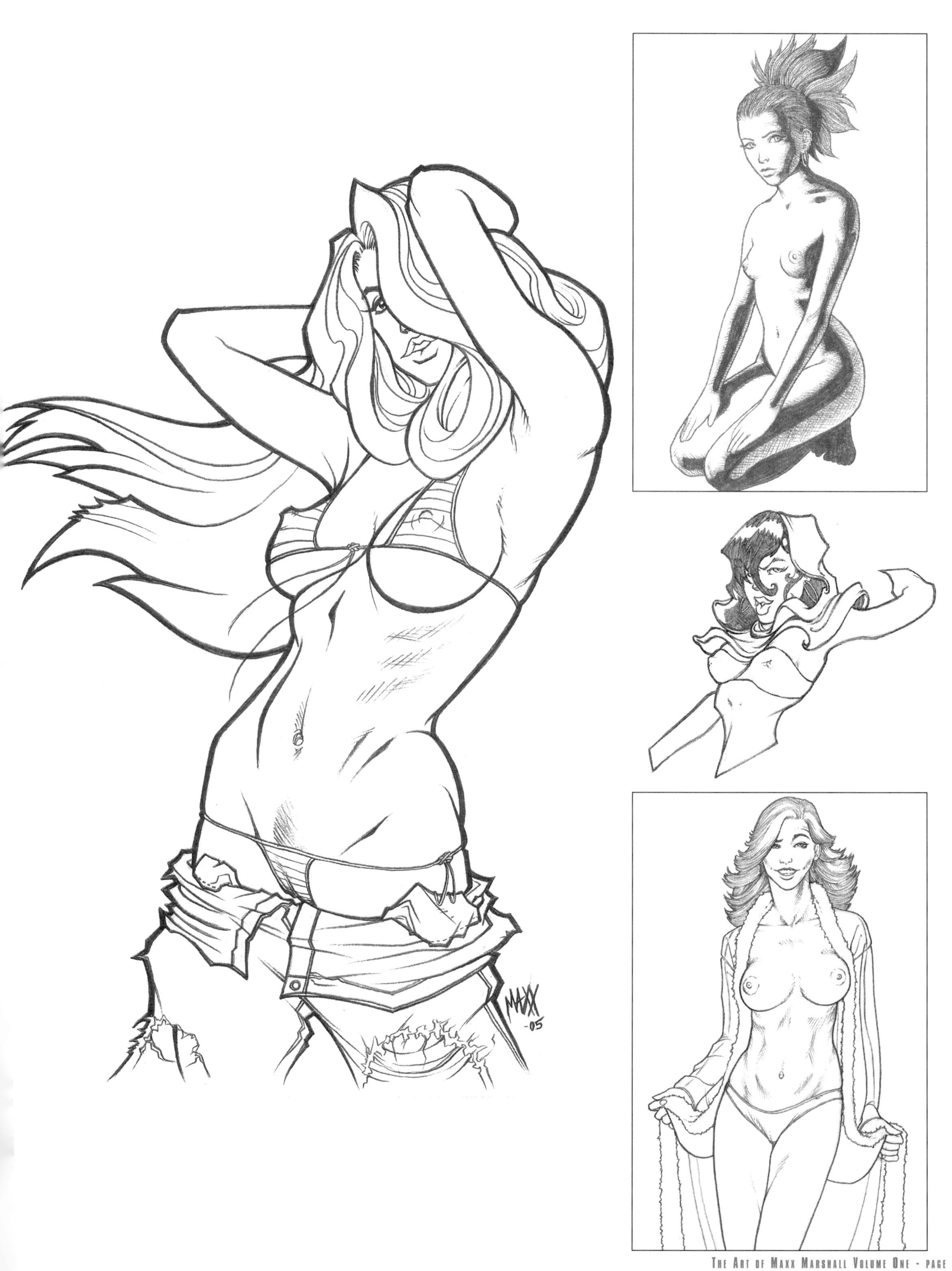
MAXX
-05

The girl getting undressed was inspired one morning by my wife. I watched as her hair was always about 2 seconds behind everything she did. It made me smile, I drew it.

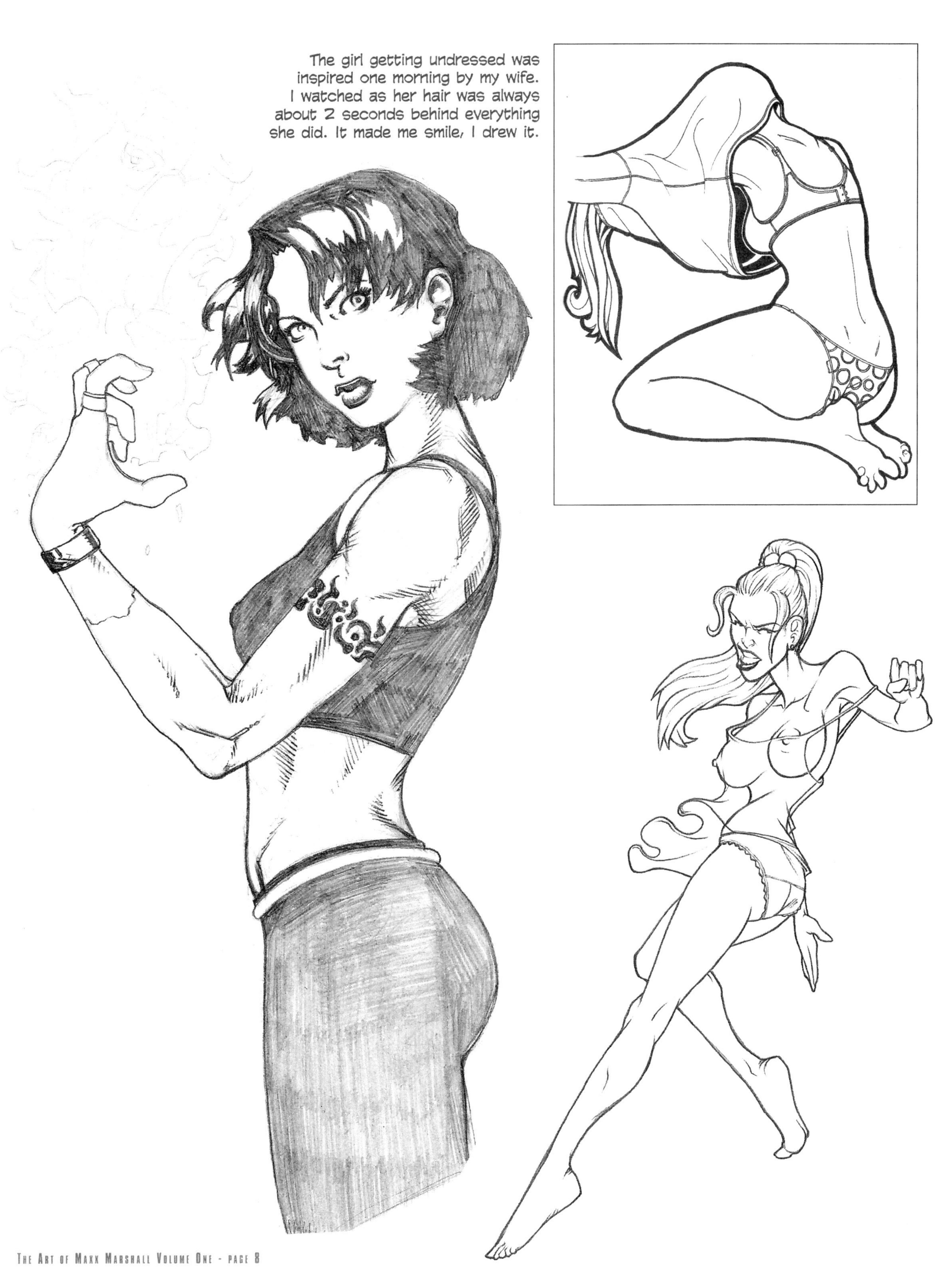

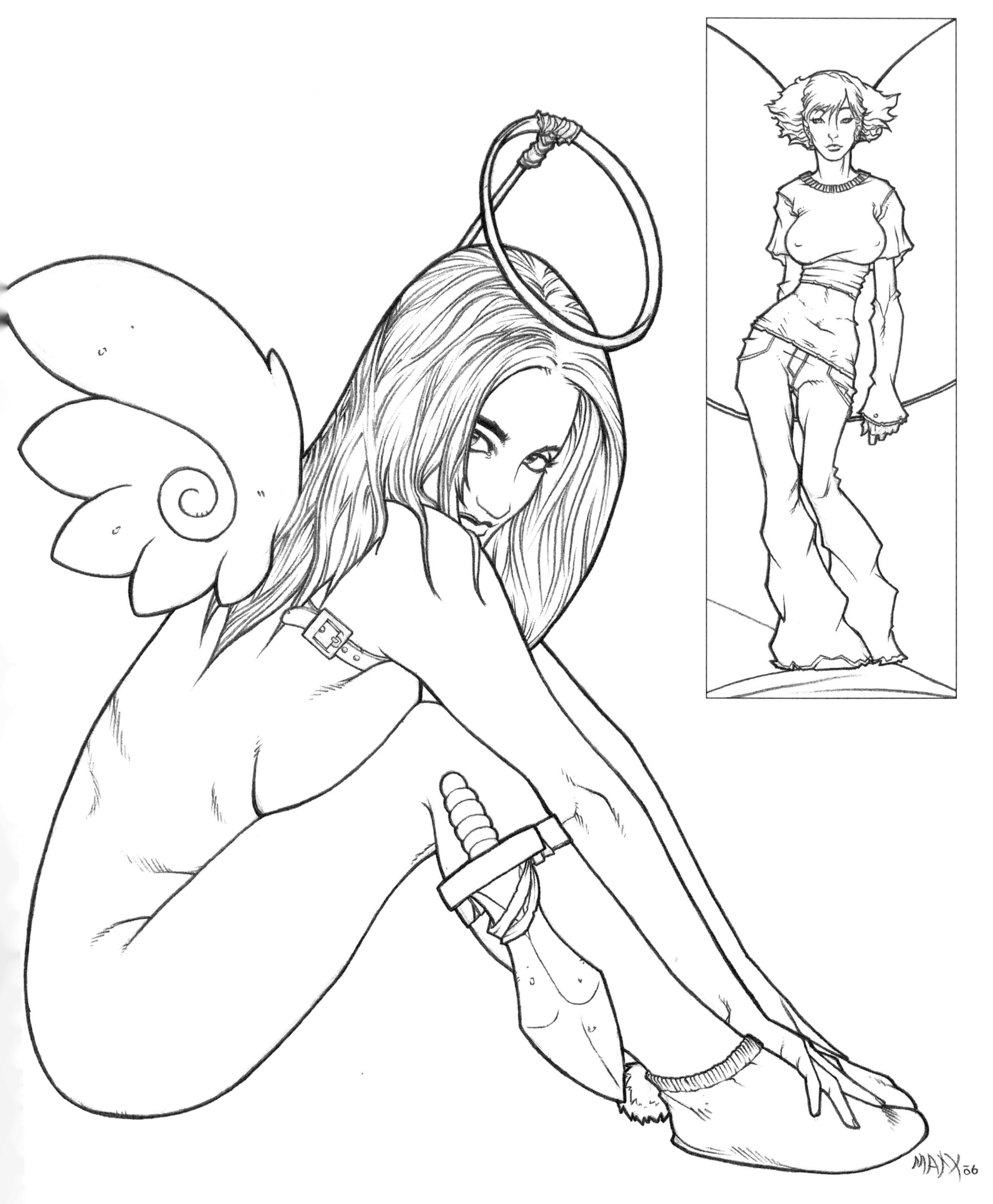
MAXX 06

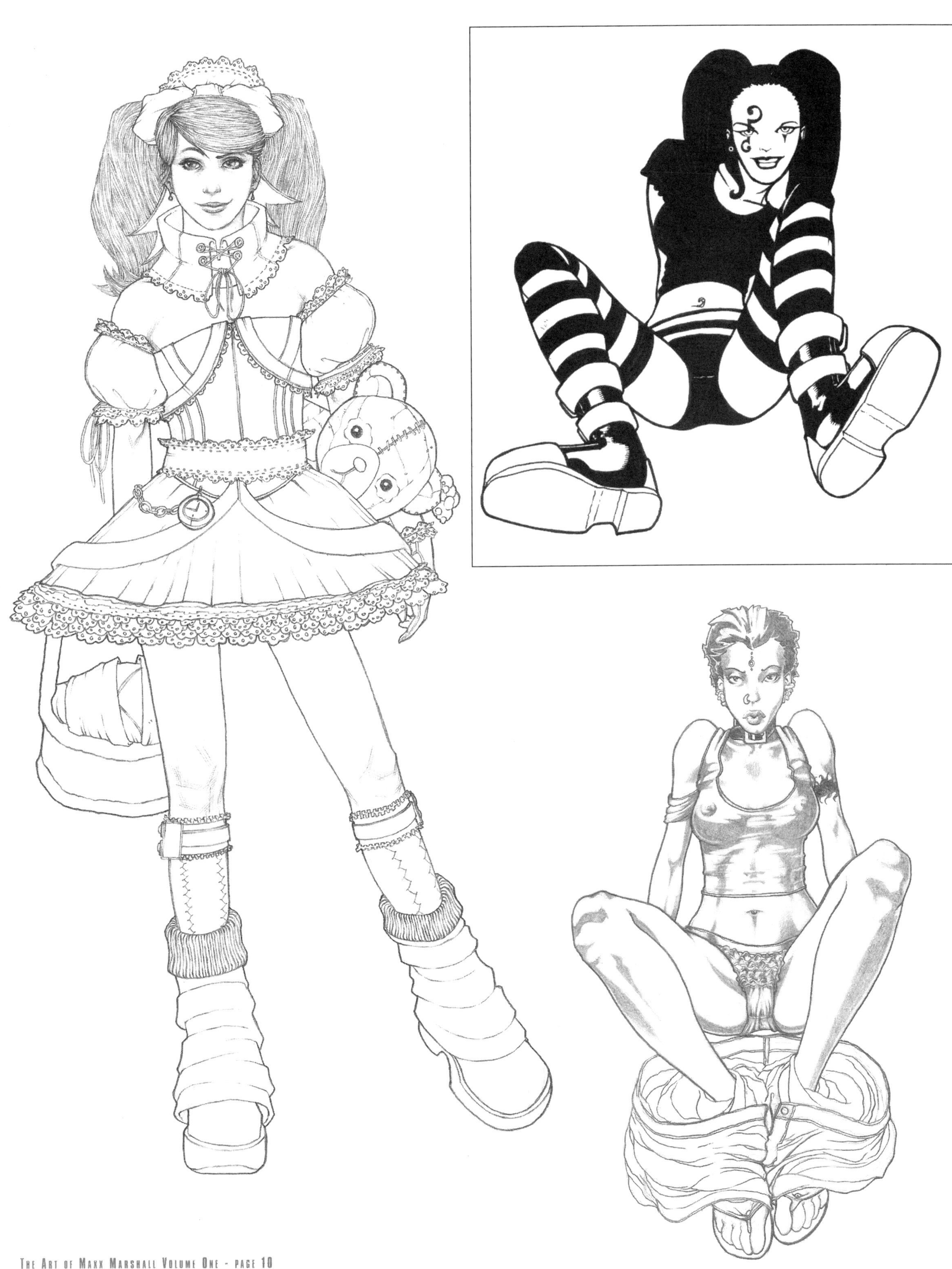

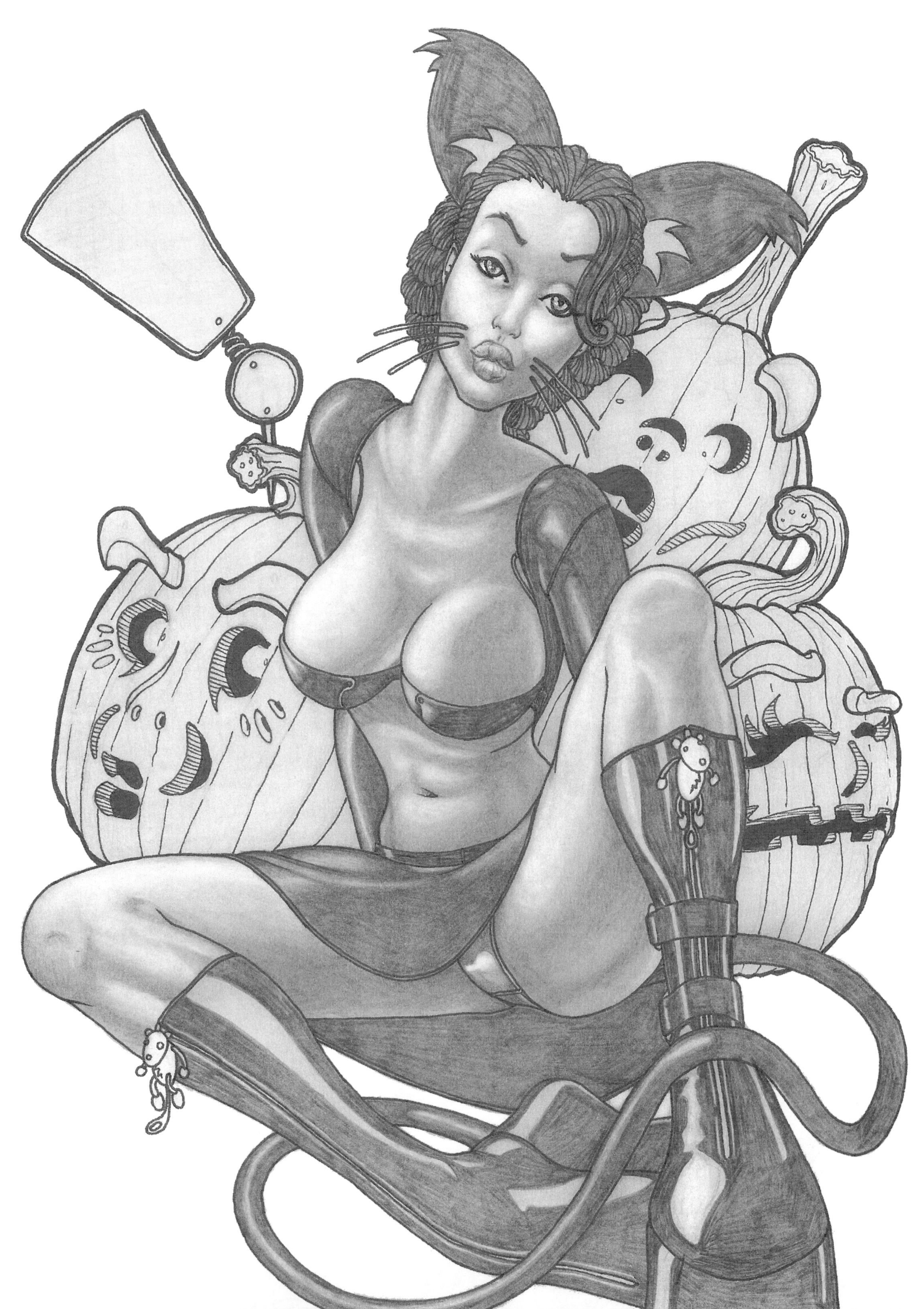

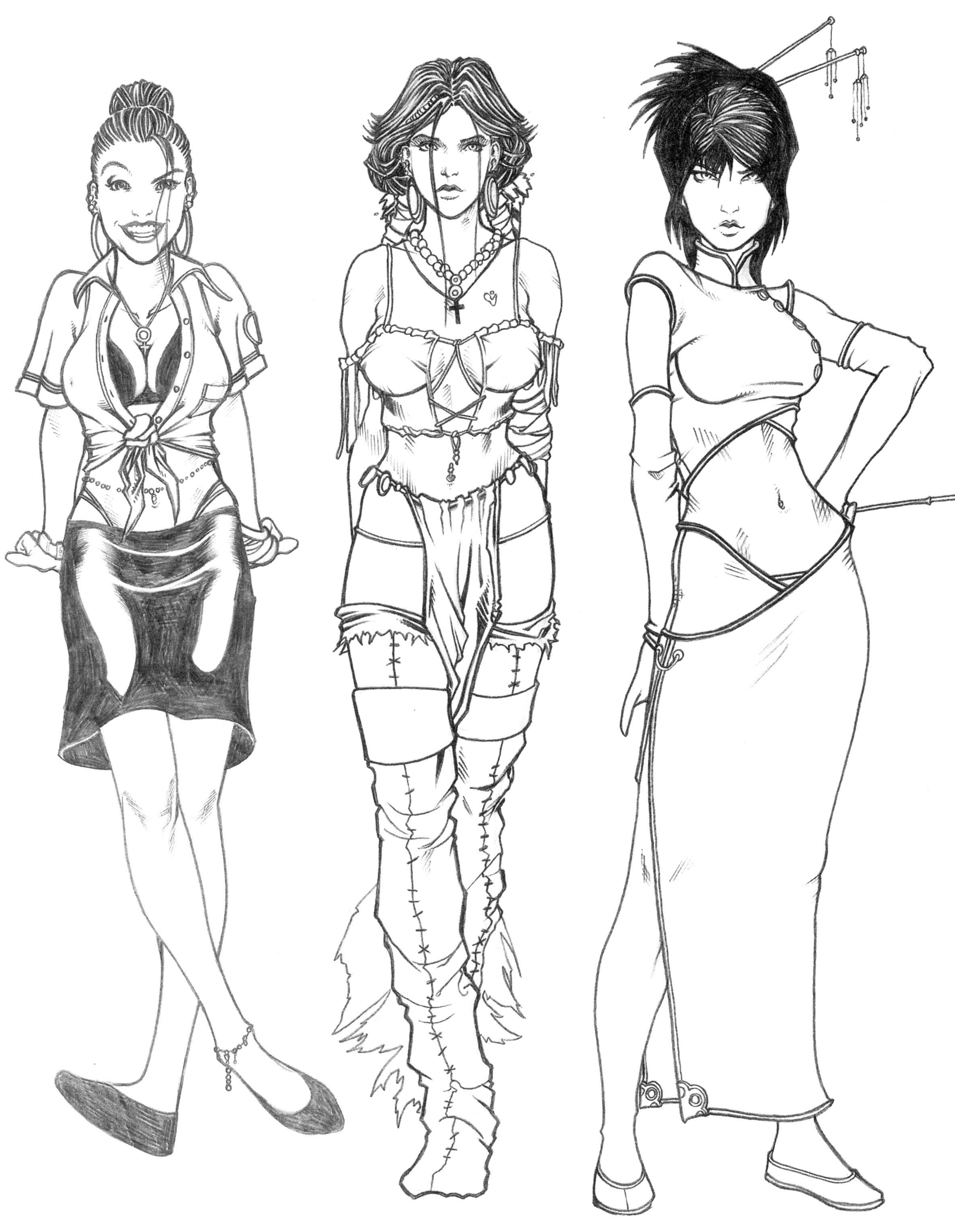

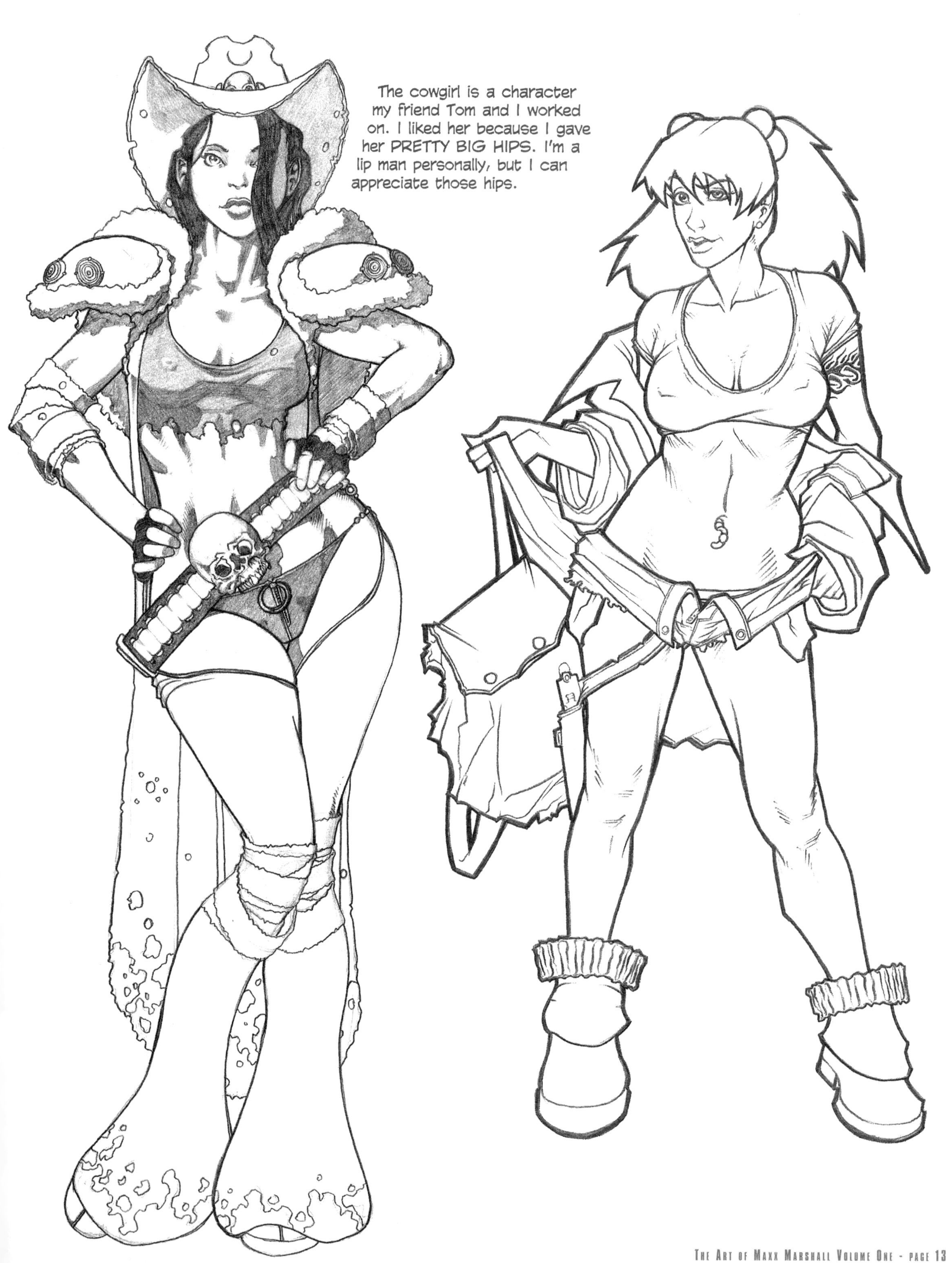

The cowgirl is a character my friend Tom and I worked on. I liked her because I gave her PRETTY BIG HIPS. I'm a lip man personally, but I can appreciate those hips.

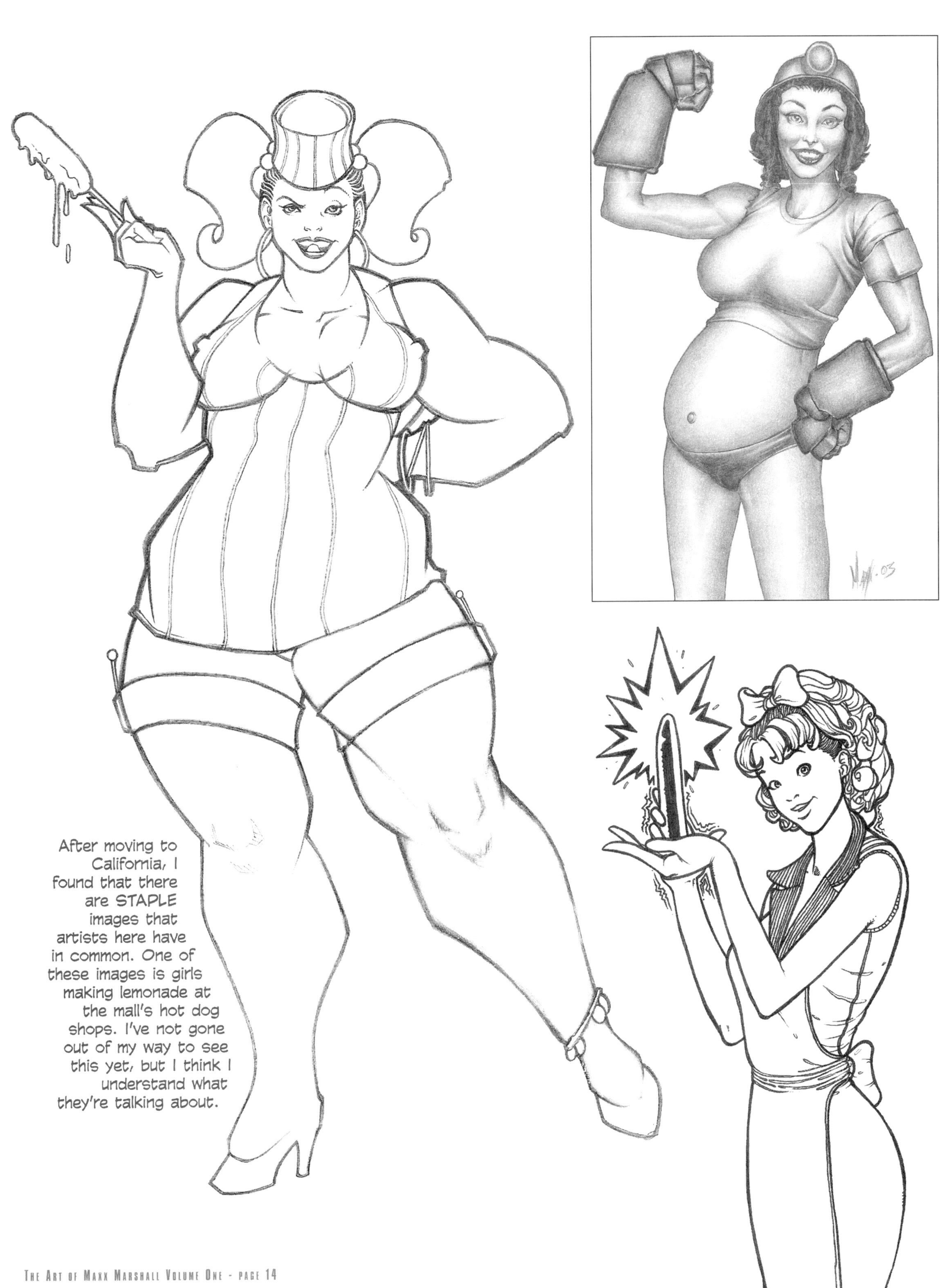

After moving to California, I found that there are STAPLE images that artists here have in common. One of these images is girls making lemonade at the mall's hot dog shops. I've not gone out of my way to see this yet, but I think I understand what they're talking about.

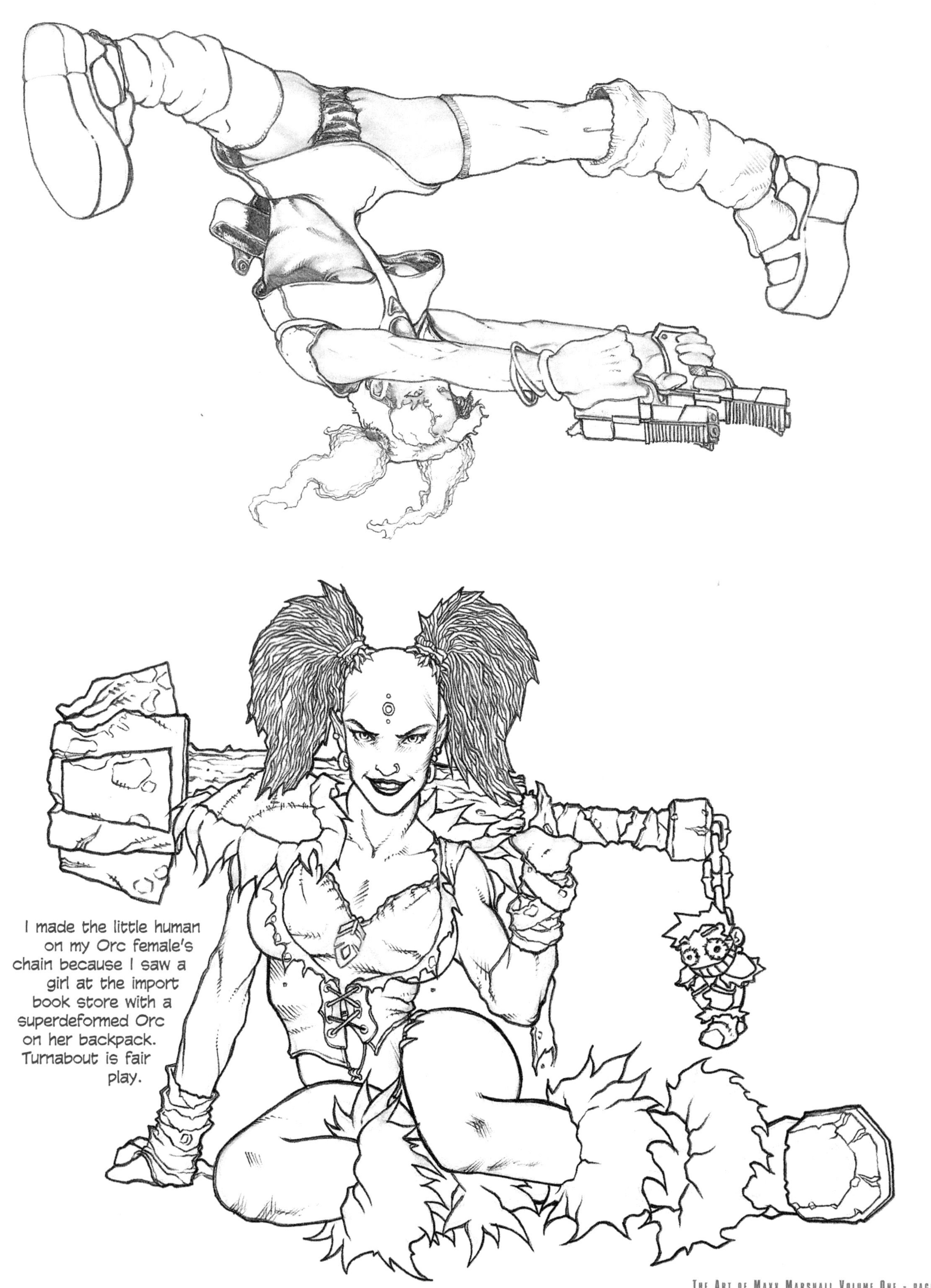

I made the little human on my Orc female's chain because I saw a girl at the import book store with a superdeformed Orc on her backpack. Turnabout is fair play.

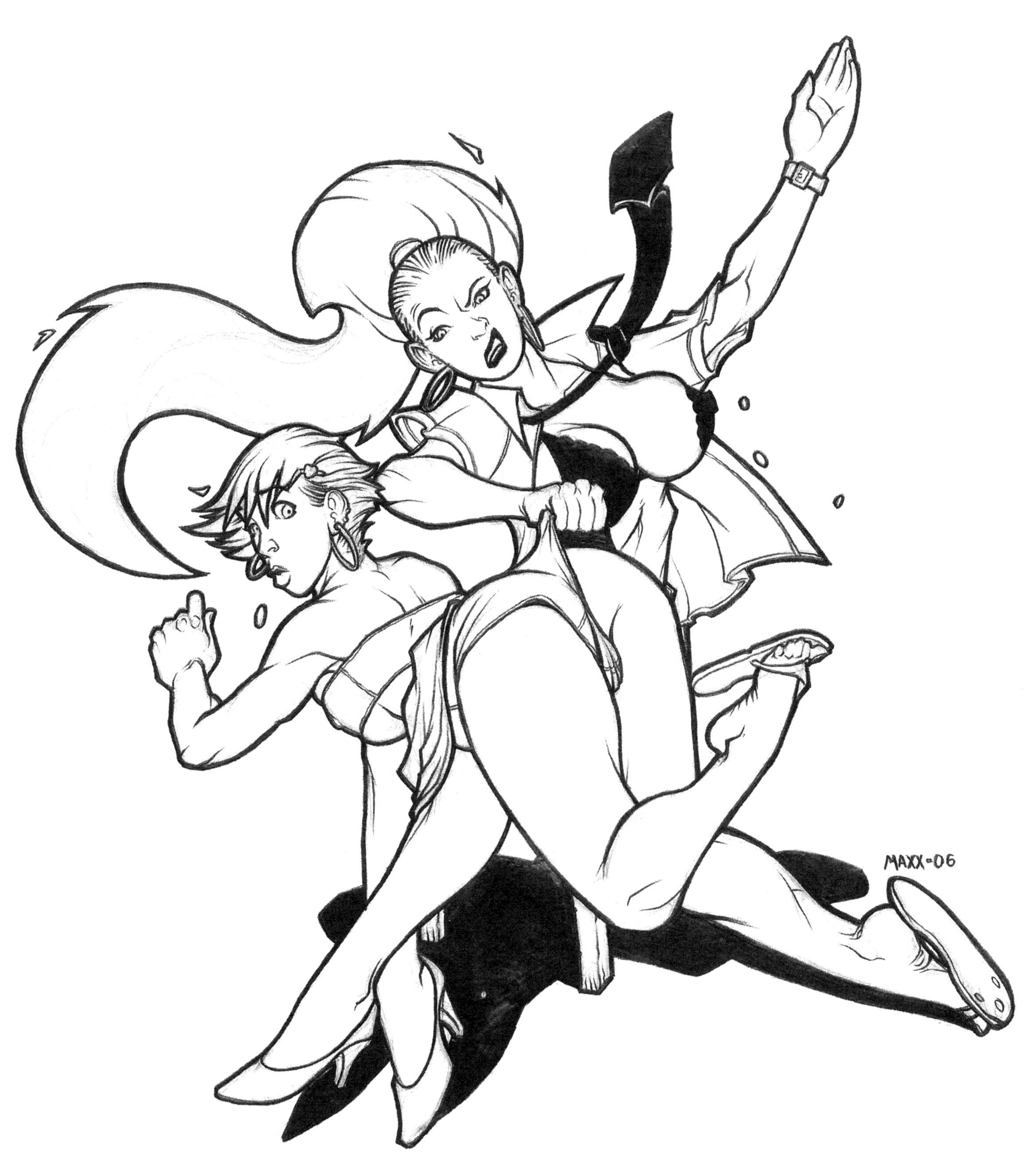
MAXX-06

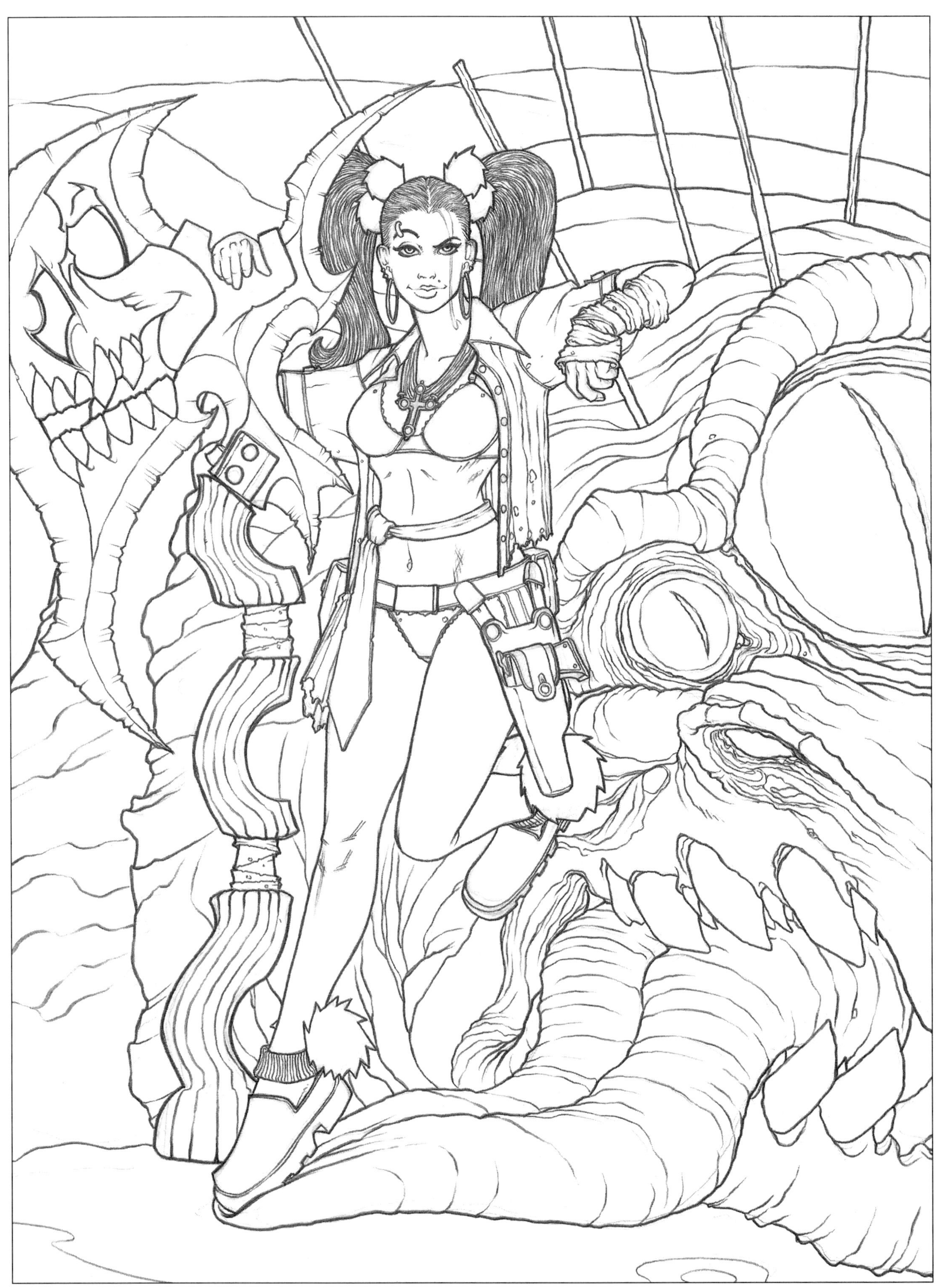

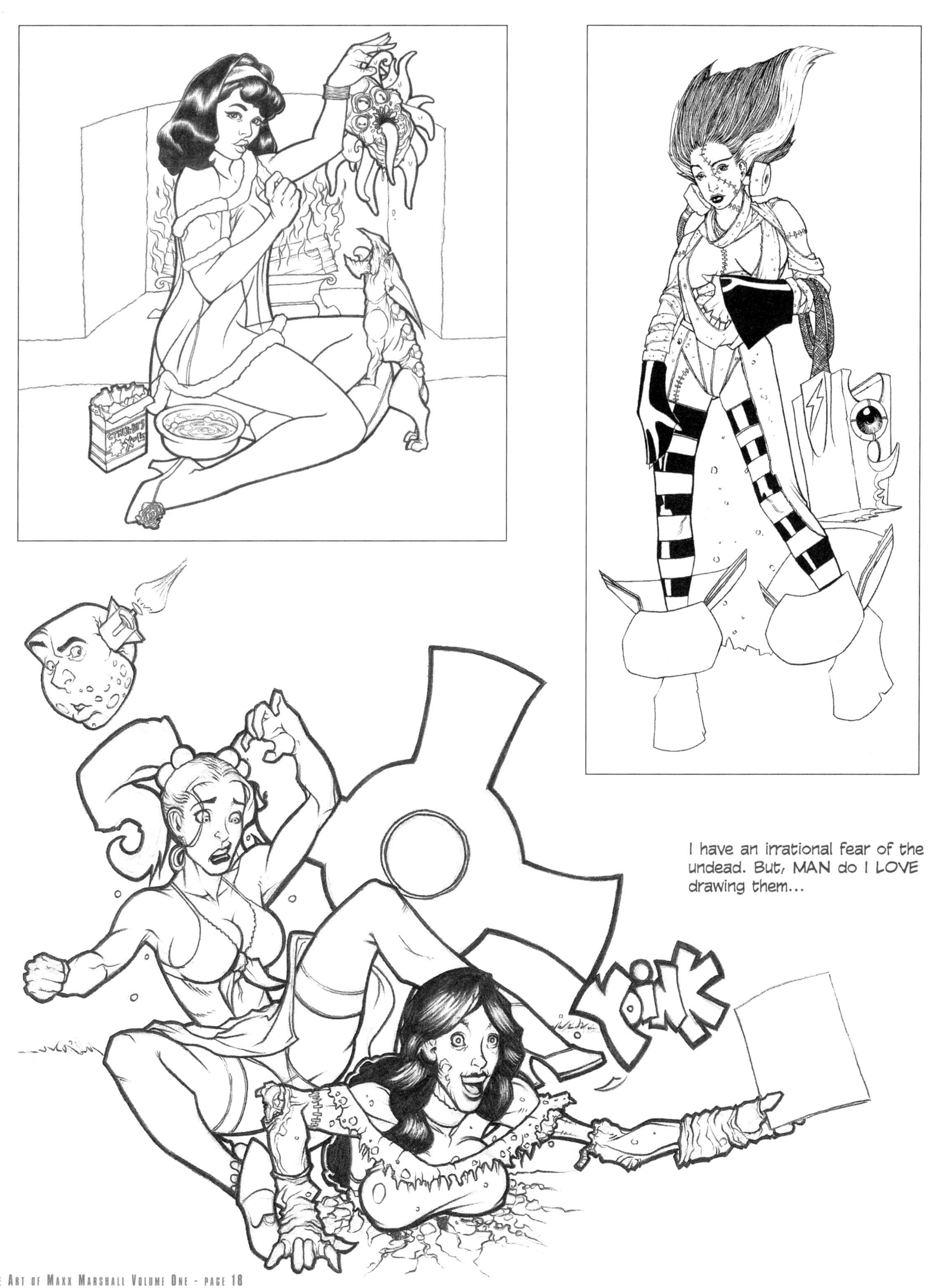

I have an irrational fear of the undead. But, MAN do I LOVE drawing them...

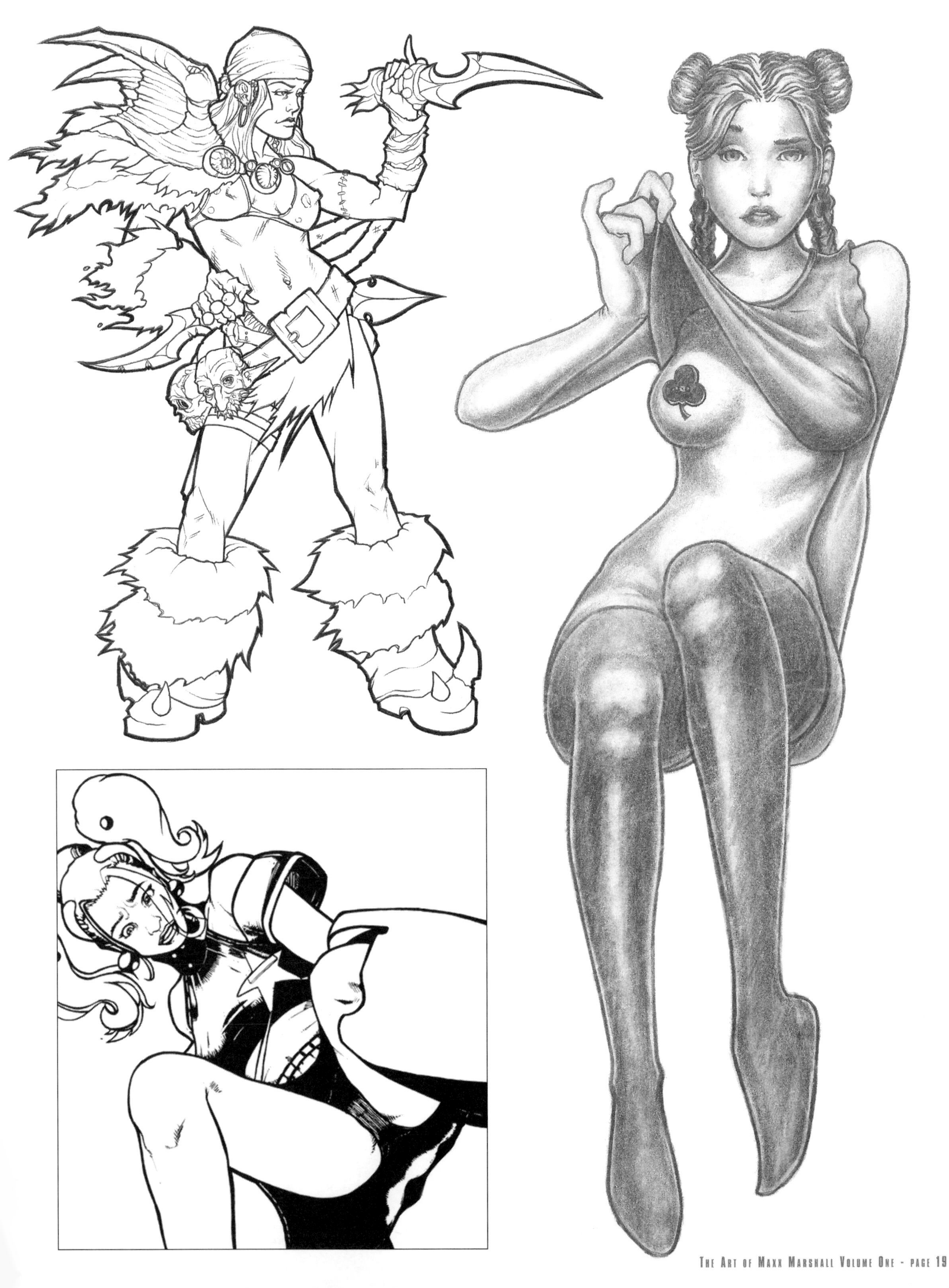

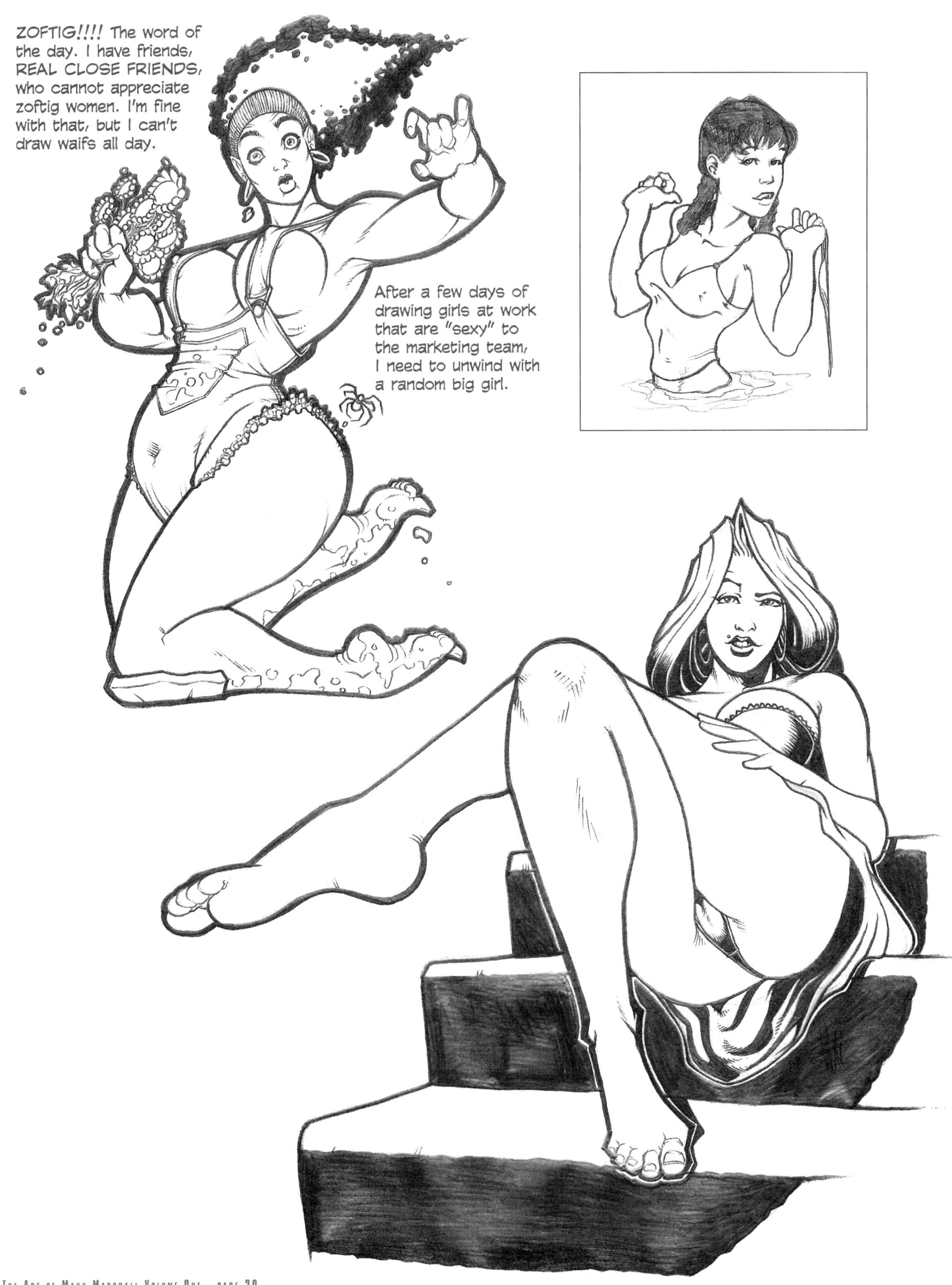

ZOFTIG!!!! The word of the day. I have friends, REAL CLOSE FRIENDS, who cannot appreciate zoftig women. I'm fine with that, but I can't draw waifs all day.

After a few days of drawing girls at work that are "sexy" to the marketing team, I need to unwind with a random big girl.

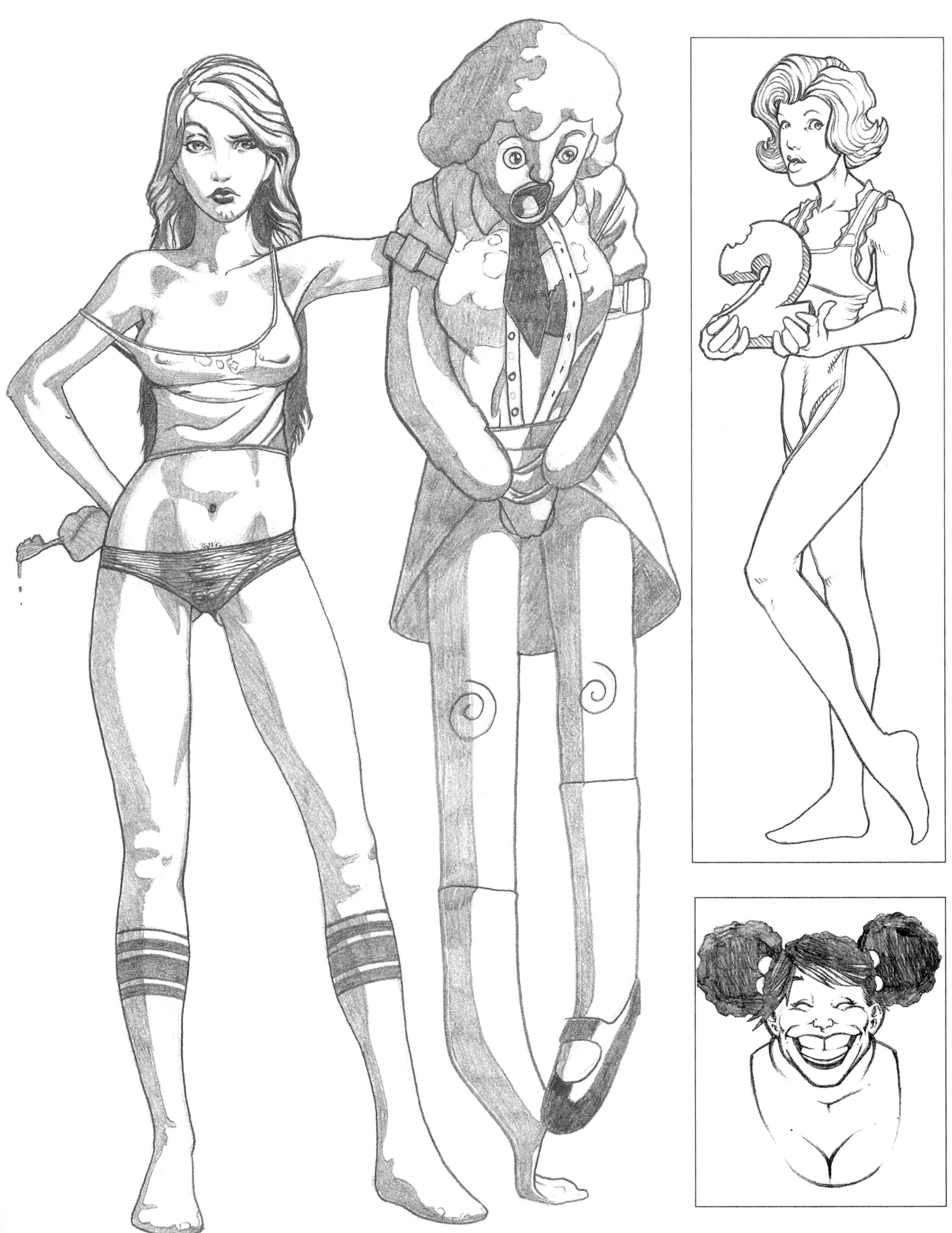

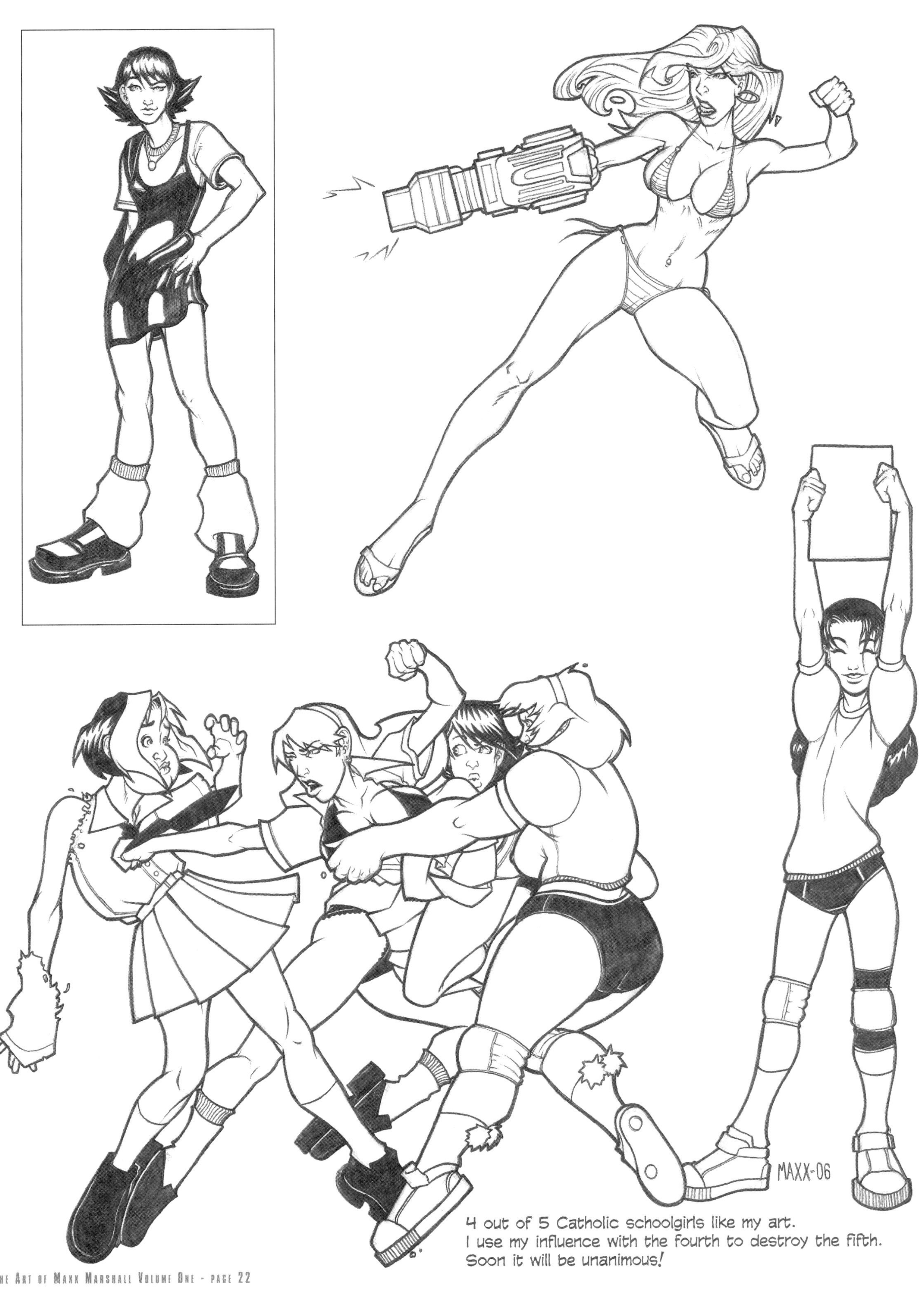

4 out of 5 Catholic schoolgirls like my art.
I use my influence with the fourth to destroy the fifth.
Soon it will be unanimous!

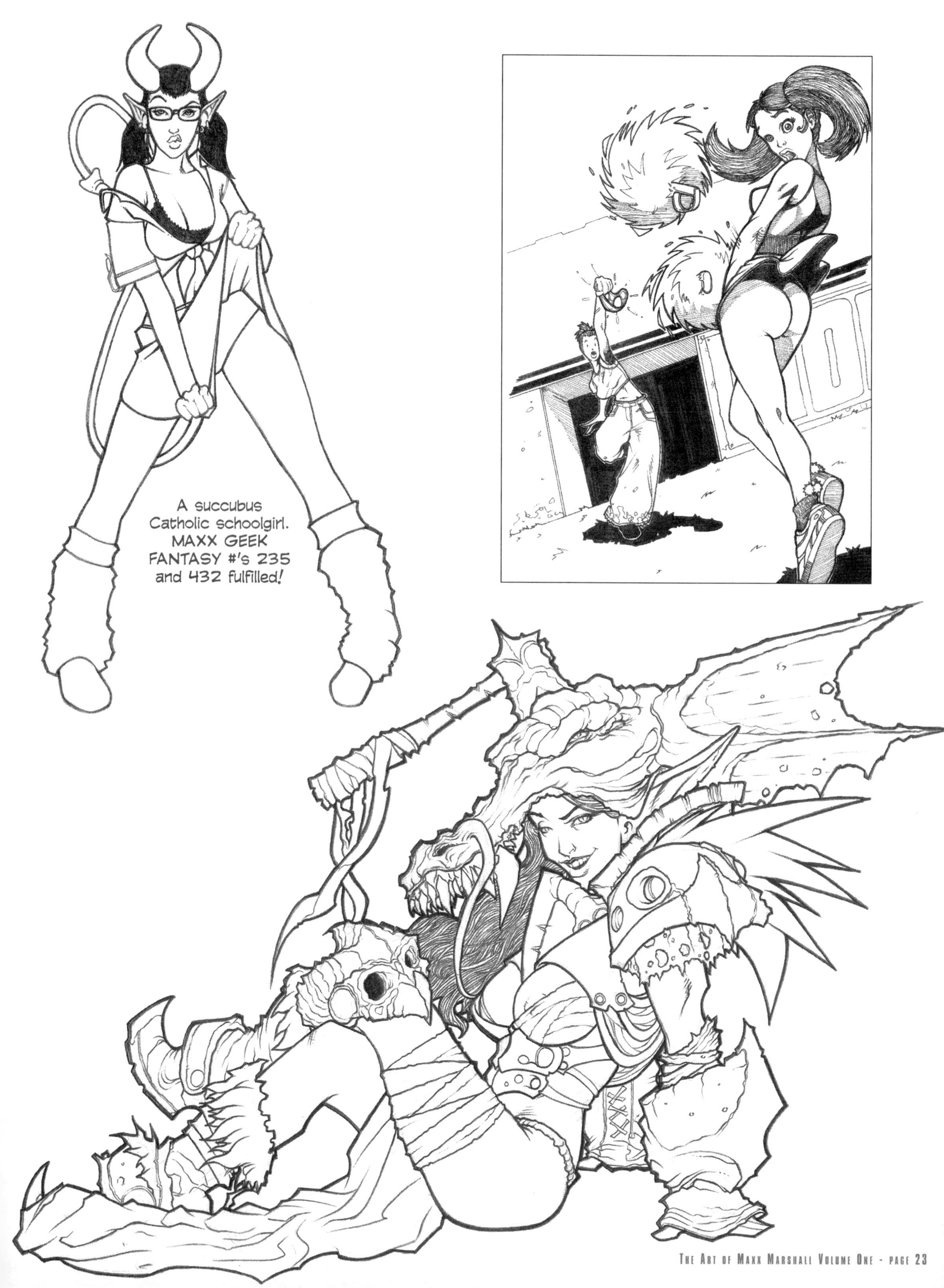
A succubus
Catholic schoolgirl.
MAXX GEEK
FANTASY #'s 235
and 432 fulfilled!

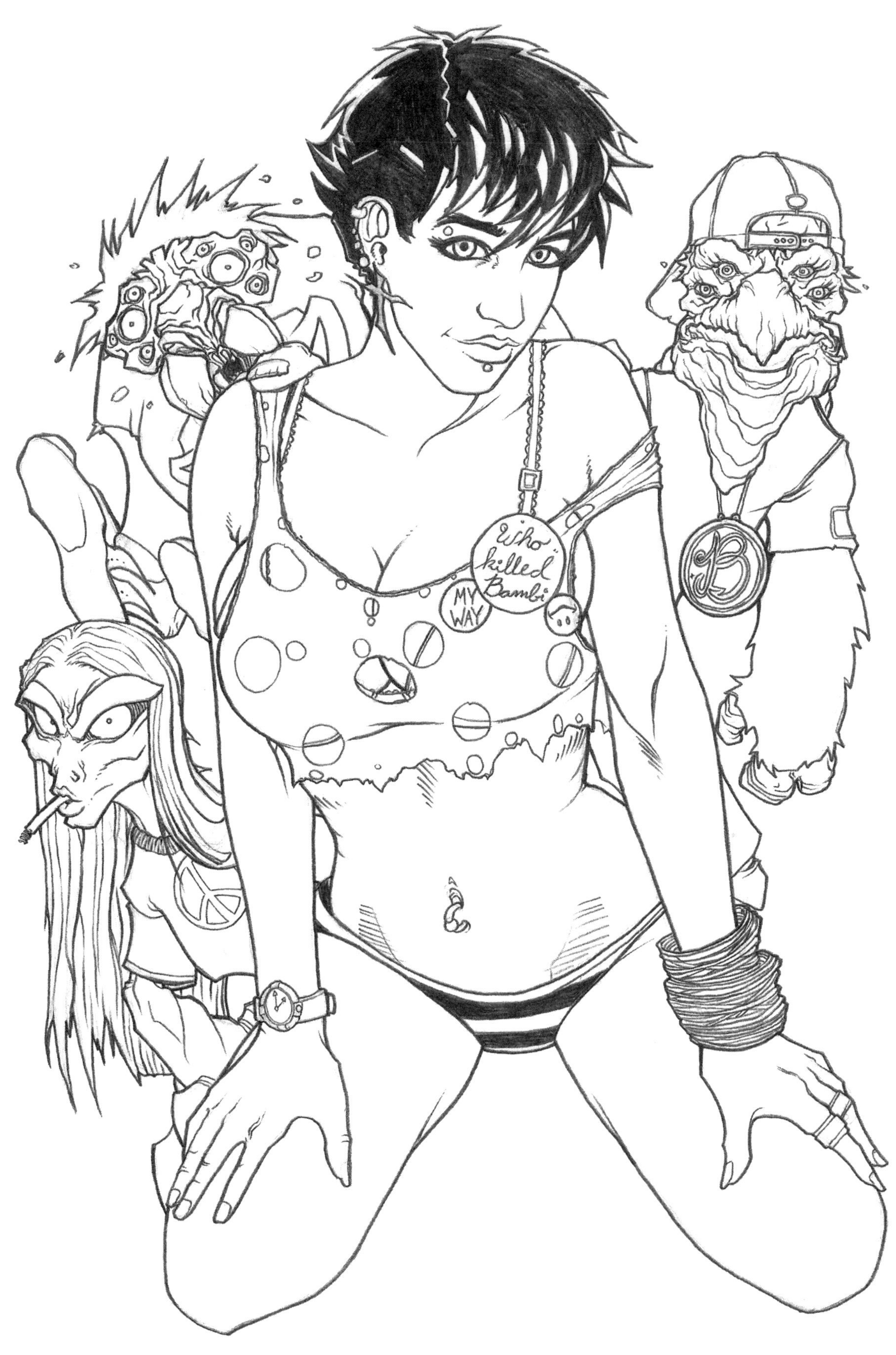
Who killed Bambi
MY WAY

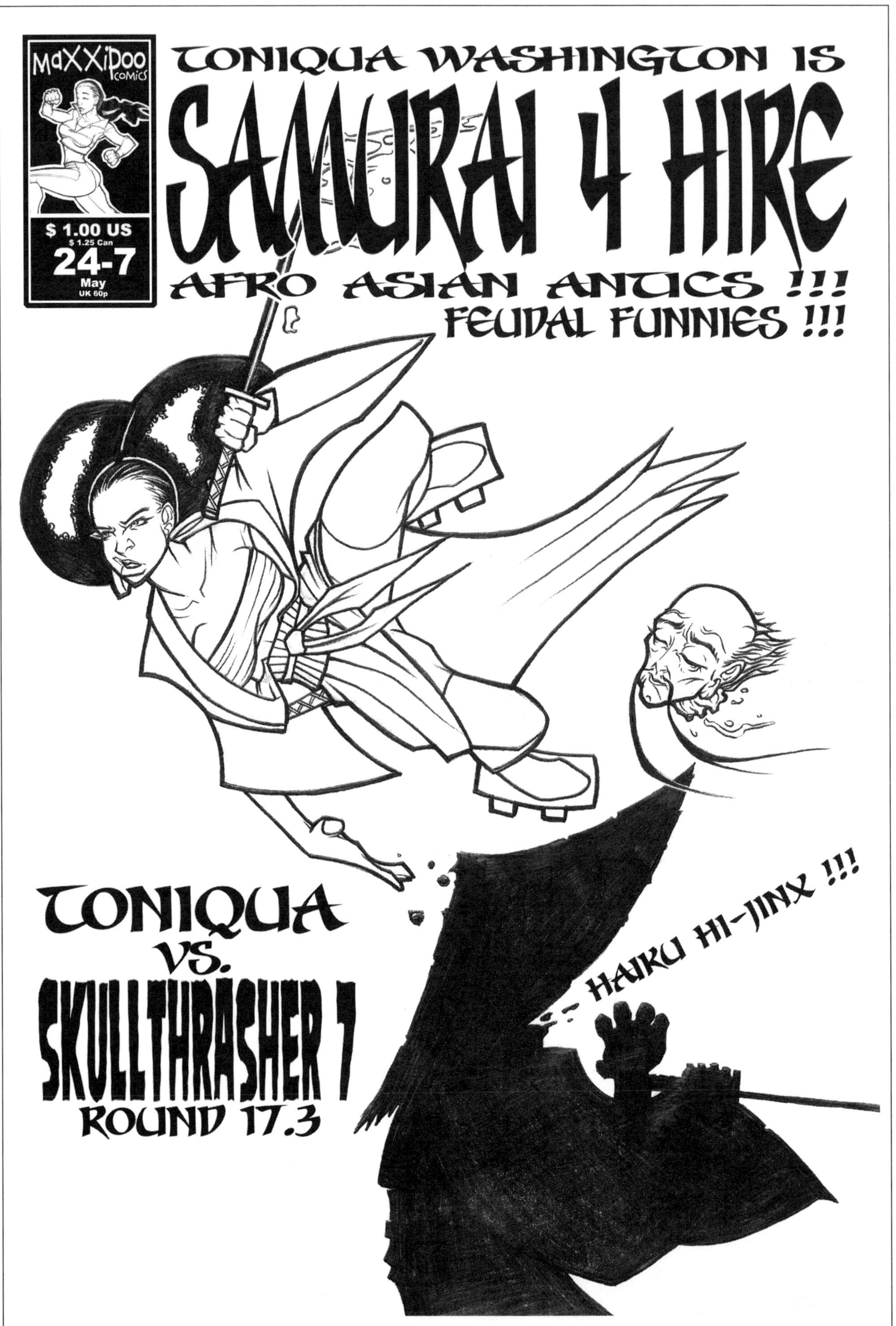
MaXXiPoo COMICS
$ 1.00 US
$ 1.25 Can
24-7
May
UK 60p
TONIQUA WASHINGTON IS
SAMURAI 4 HIRE
AFRO ASIAN ANTICS !!!
FEUDAL FUNNIES !!!
TONIQUA
VS.
SKULLTHRASHER 7
ROUND 17.3
HAIKU HI-JINX !!!

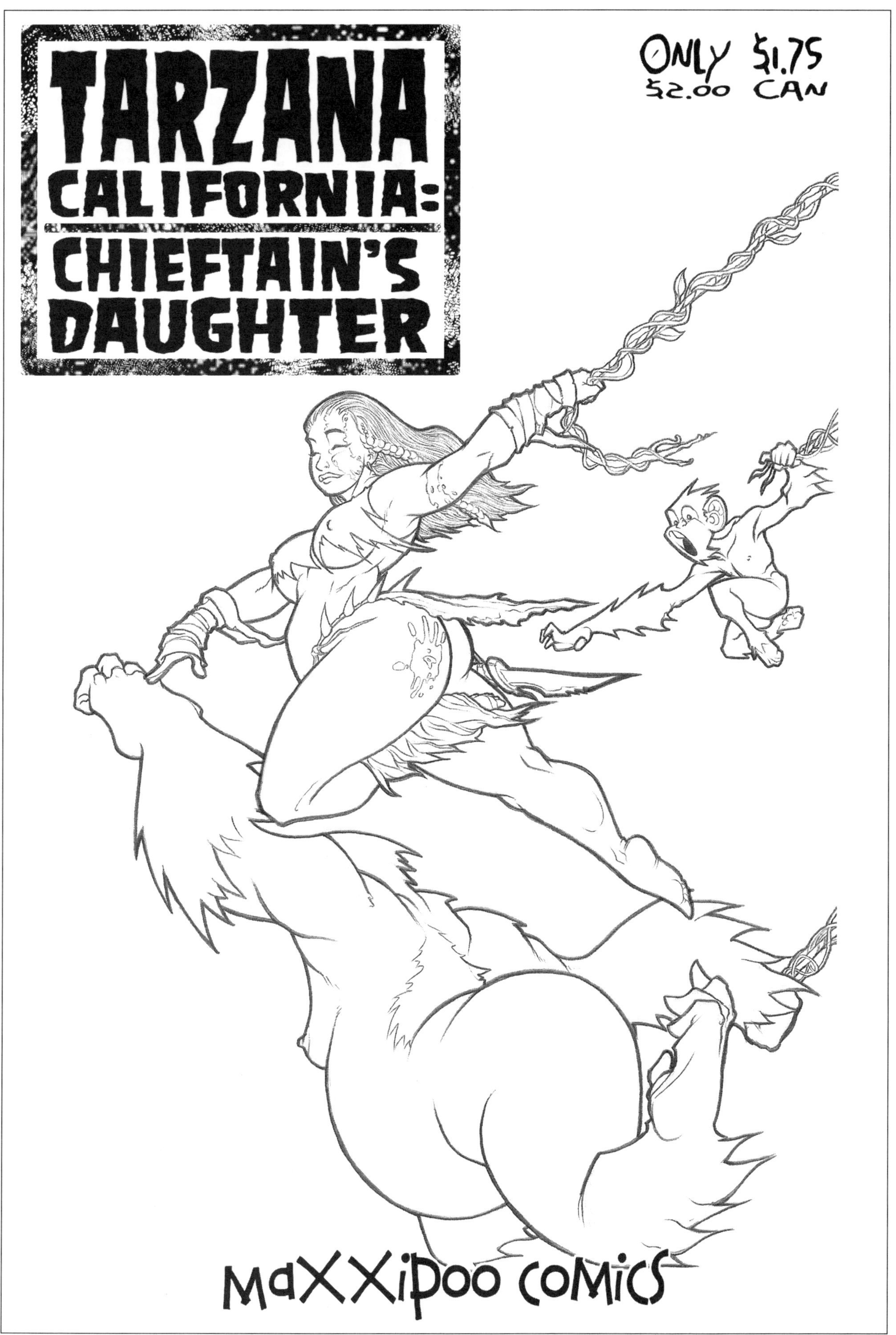
TARZANA
CALIFORNIA:
CHIEFTAIN'S
DAUGHTER
ONLY $1.75
$2.00 CAN
MaXXiPoo COMICS

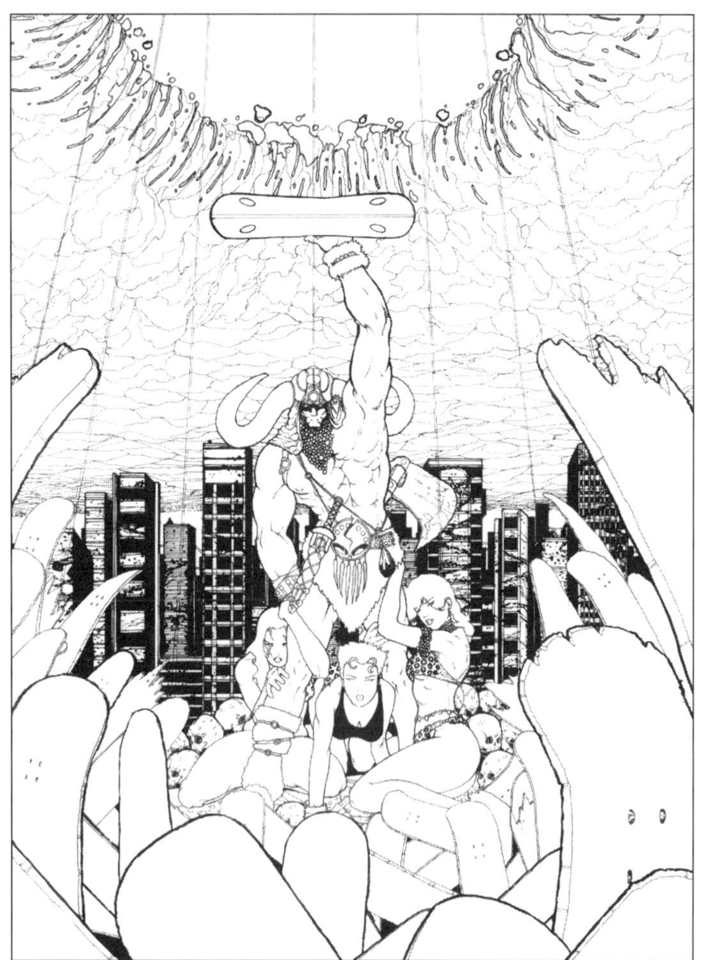

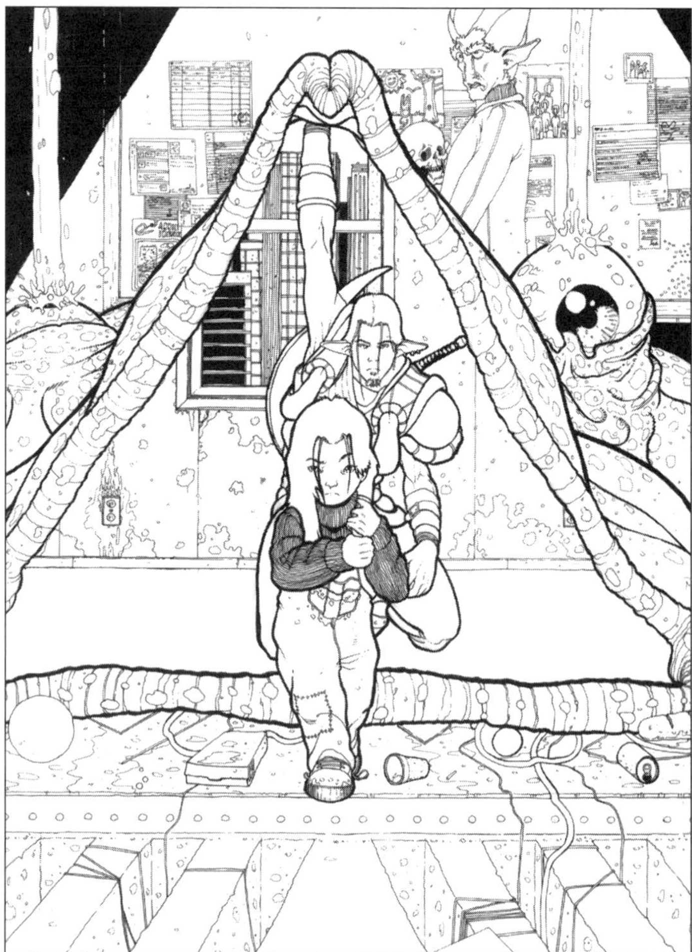

This bottom image is my buddy Carlo and I doing battle on a day time talk show. I KNOW I'd win this battle because he'd get distracted by the girl in the back.....actually so would I, so it'd be a draw.

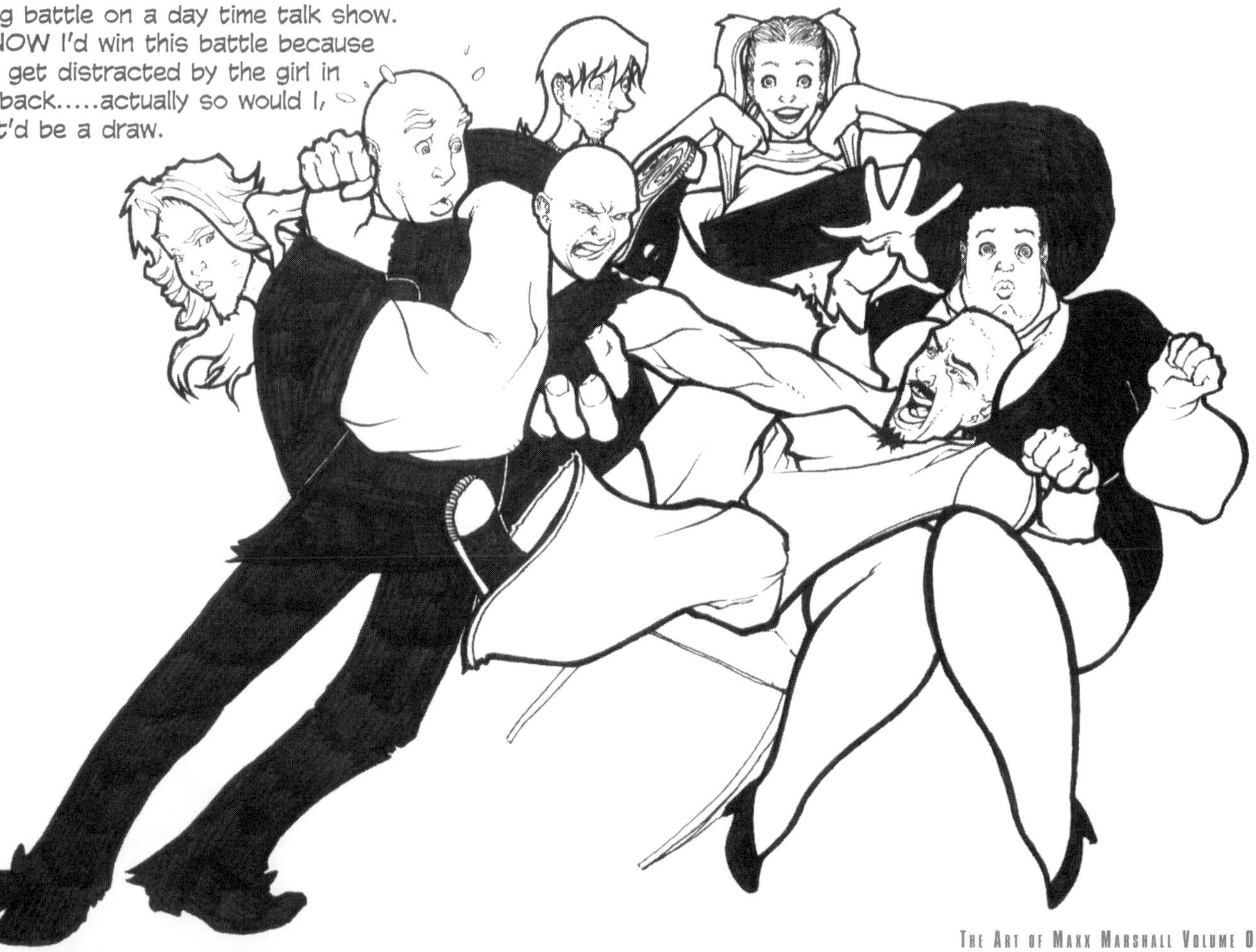

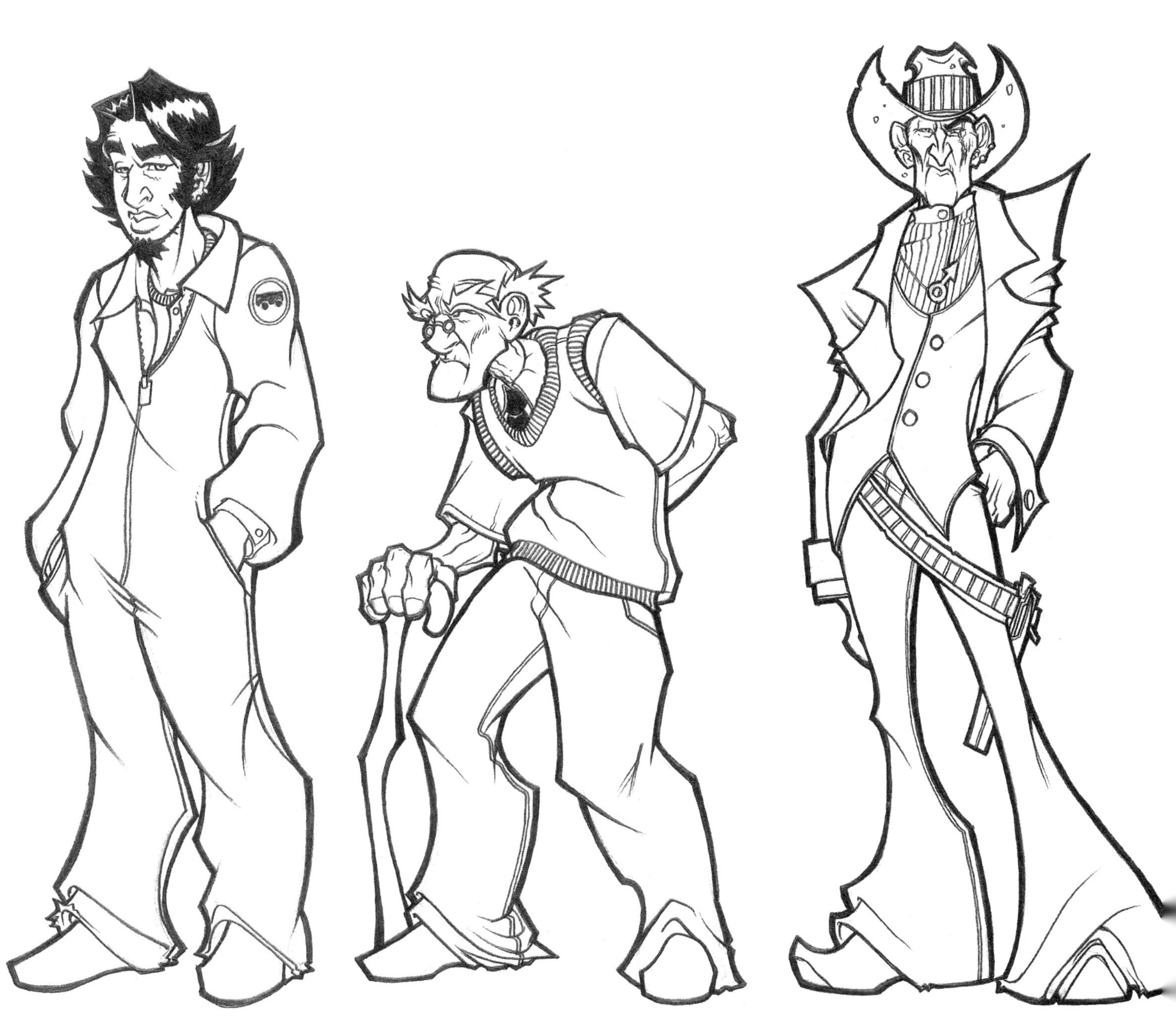

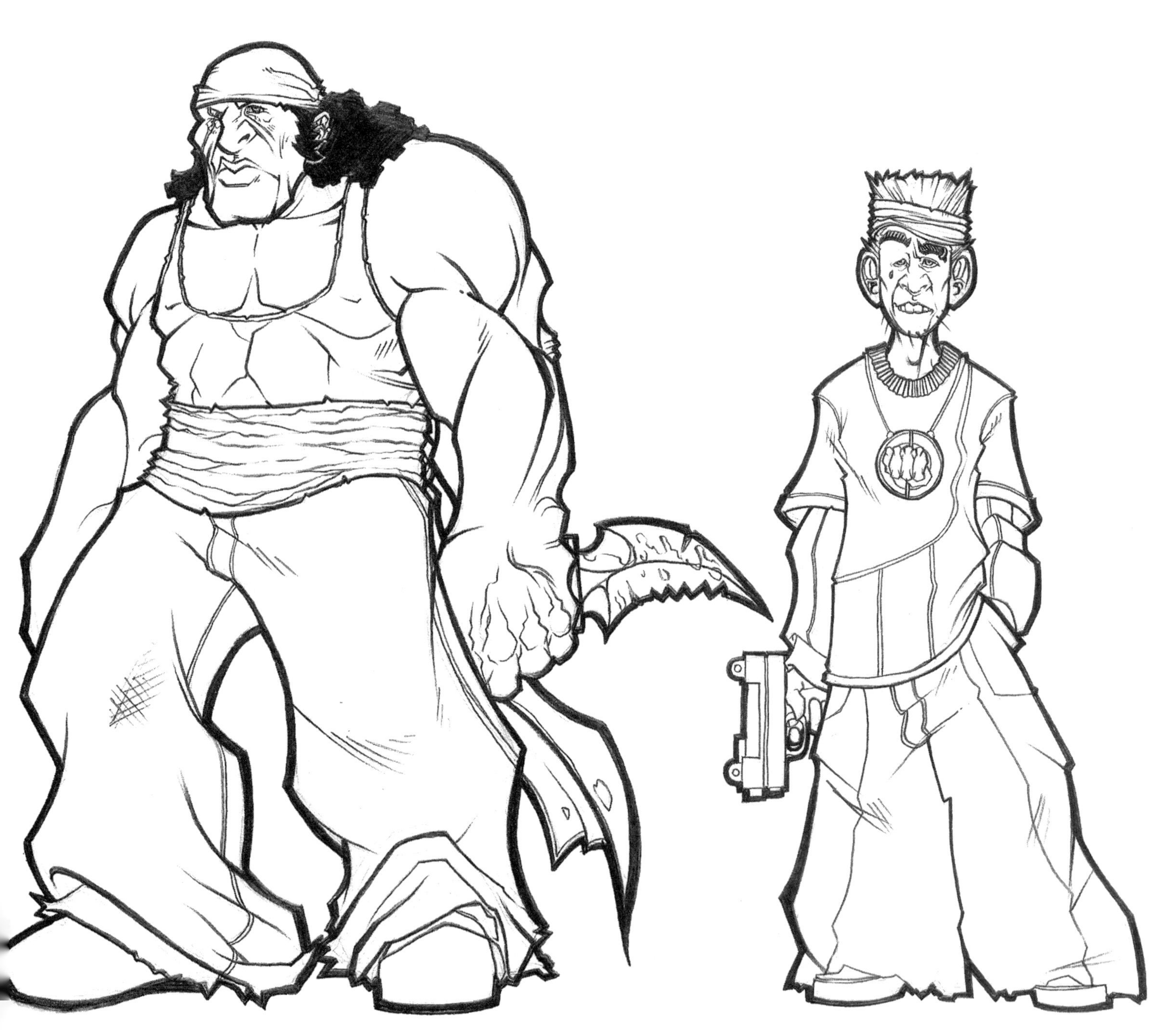

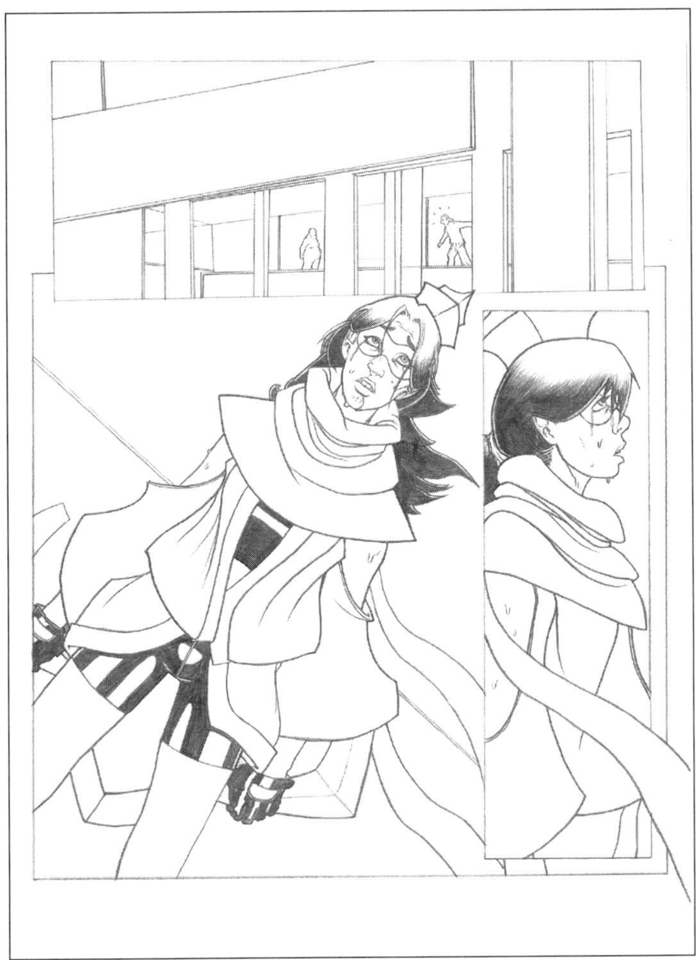

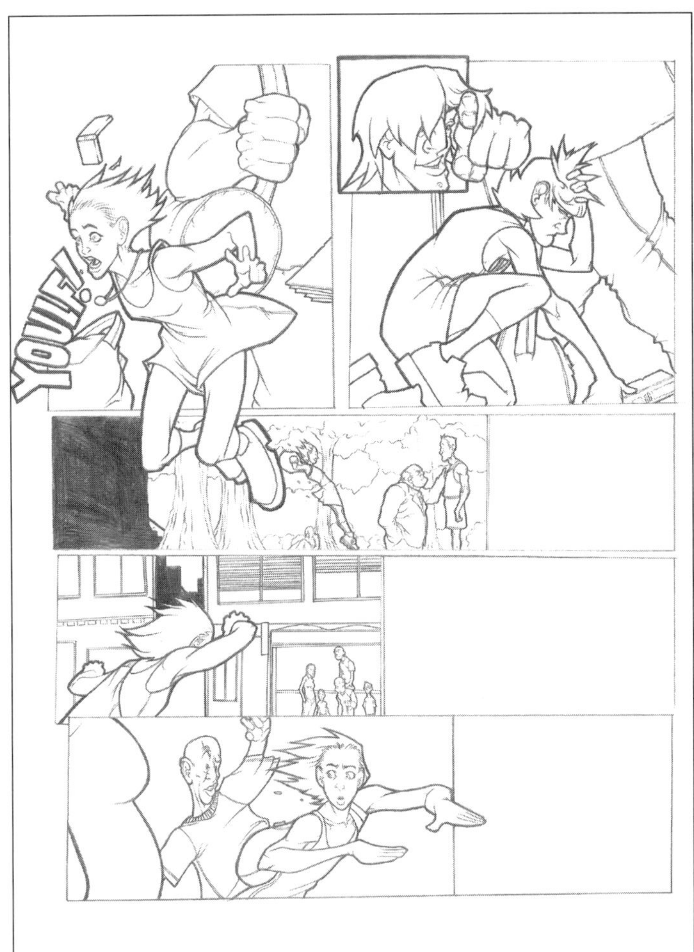

YOUFF!

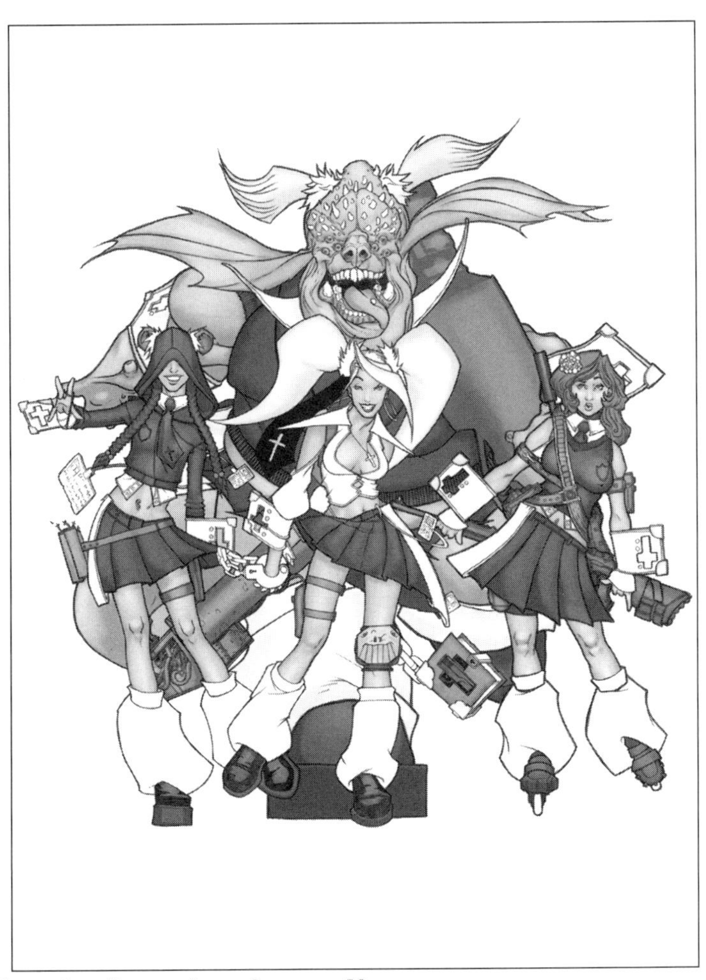

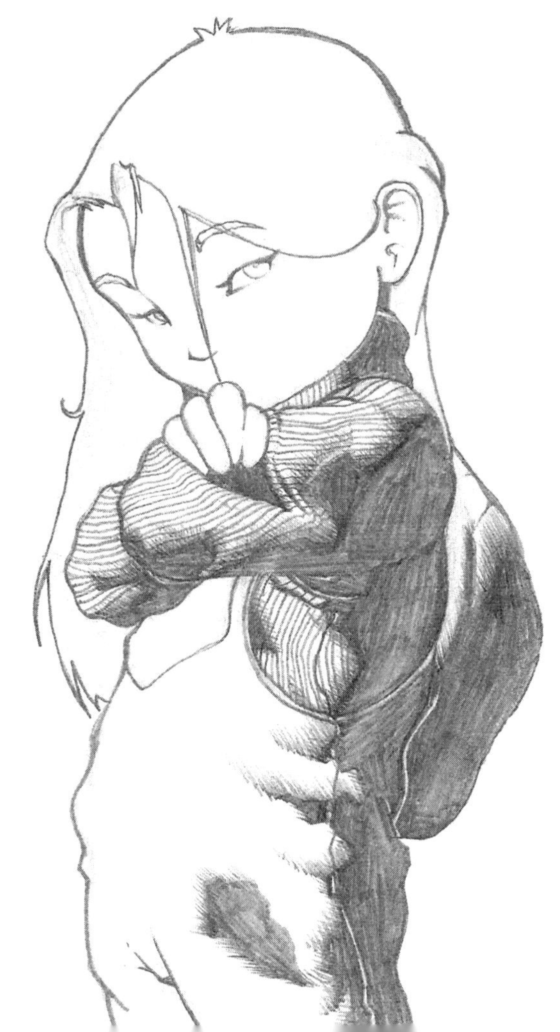

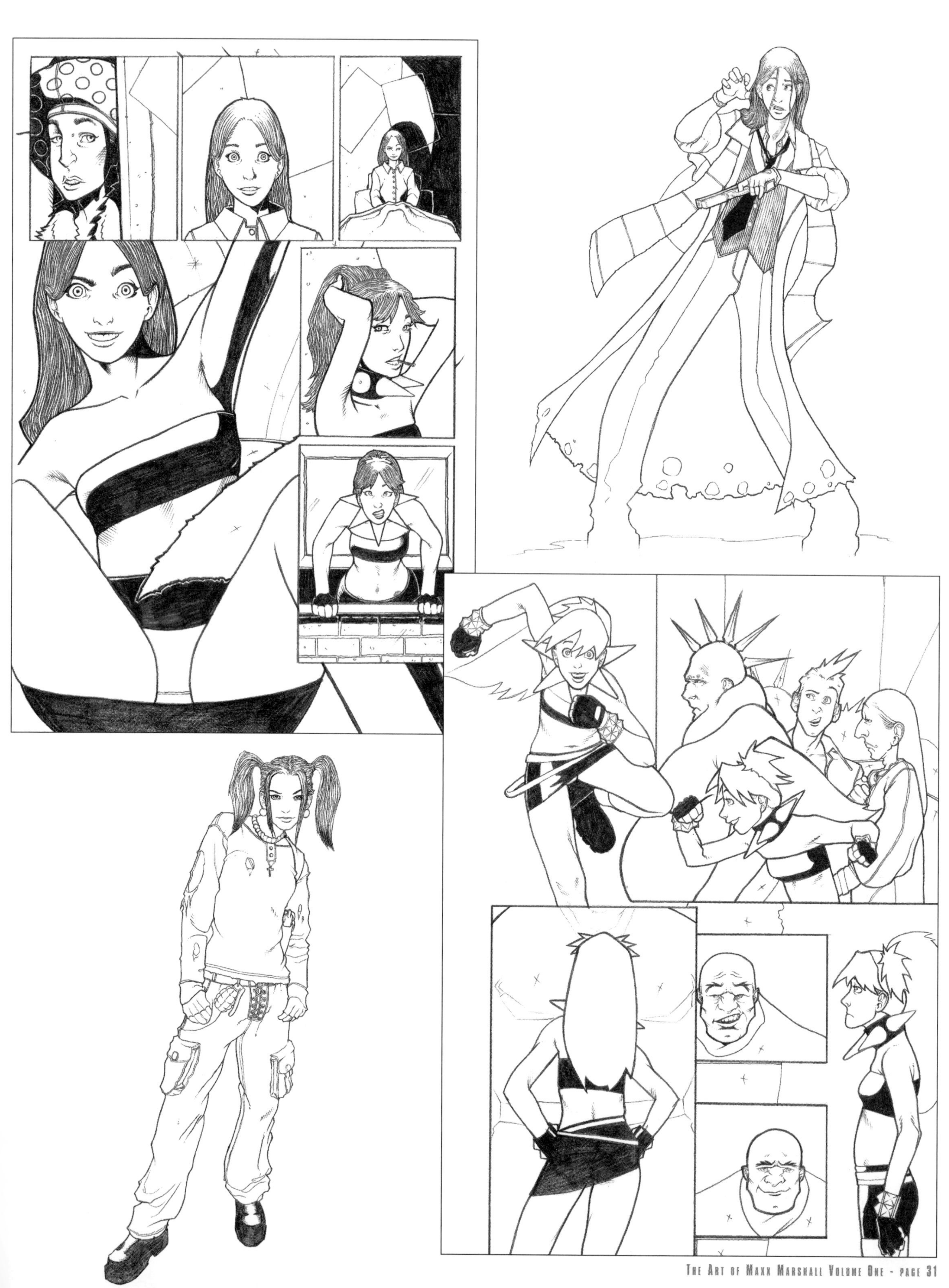

I drew this after playing a game with a rather good character editor. I made her, and played through the game with her. After the game was done, I wanted to keep drawing her. Note that MY backpack is often in my art. (below her) I buy the exact same backpack every couple of years. I've probably drawn it over a thousand times now.

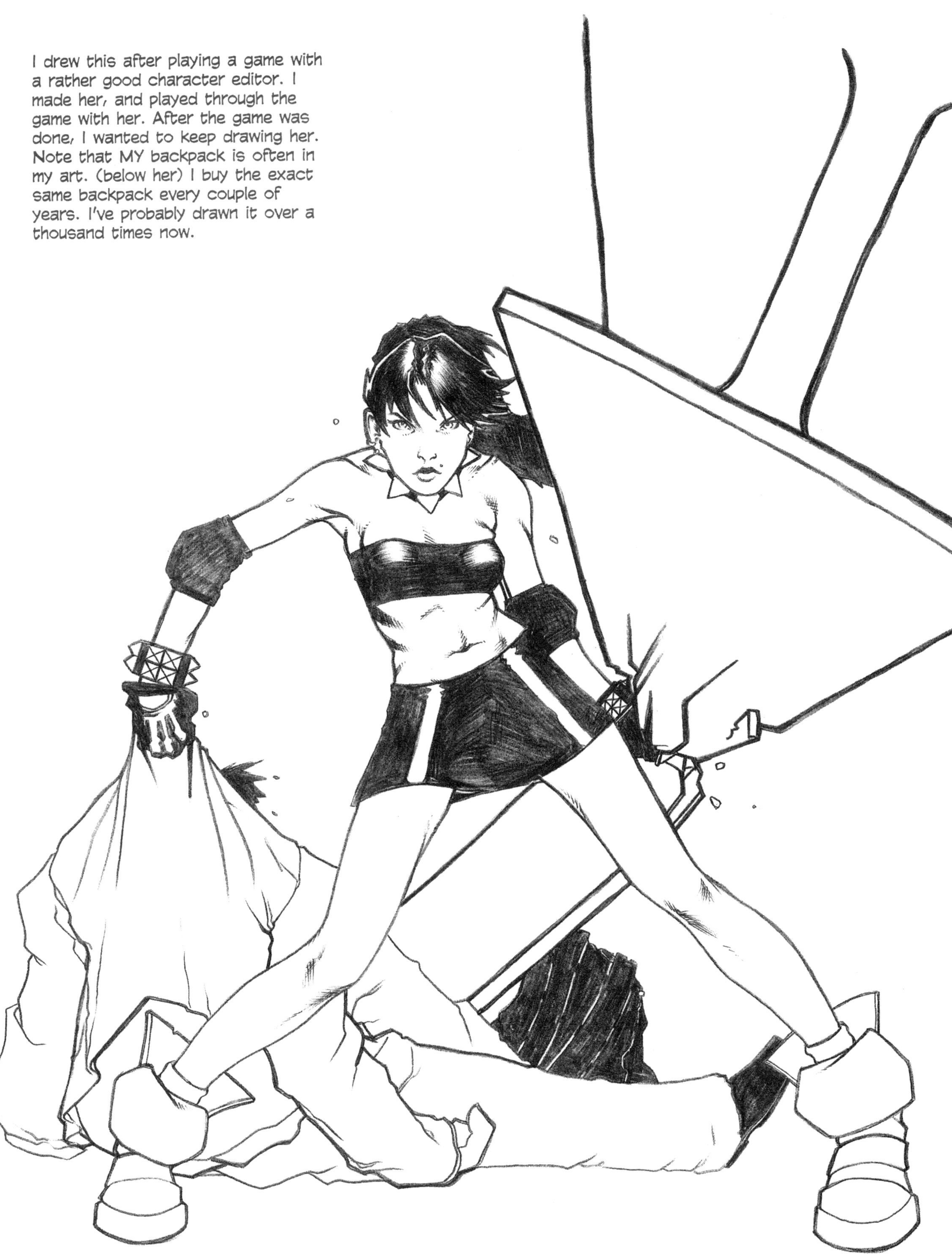

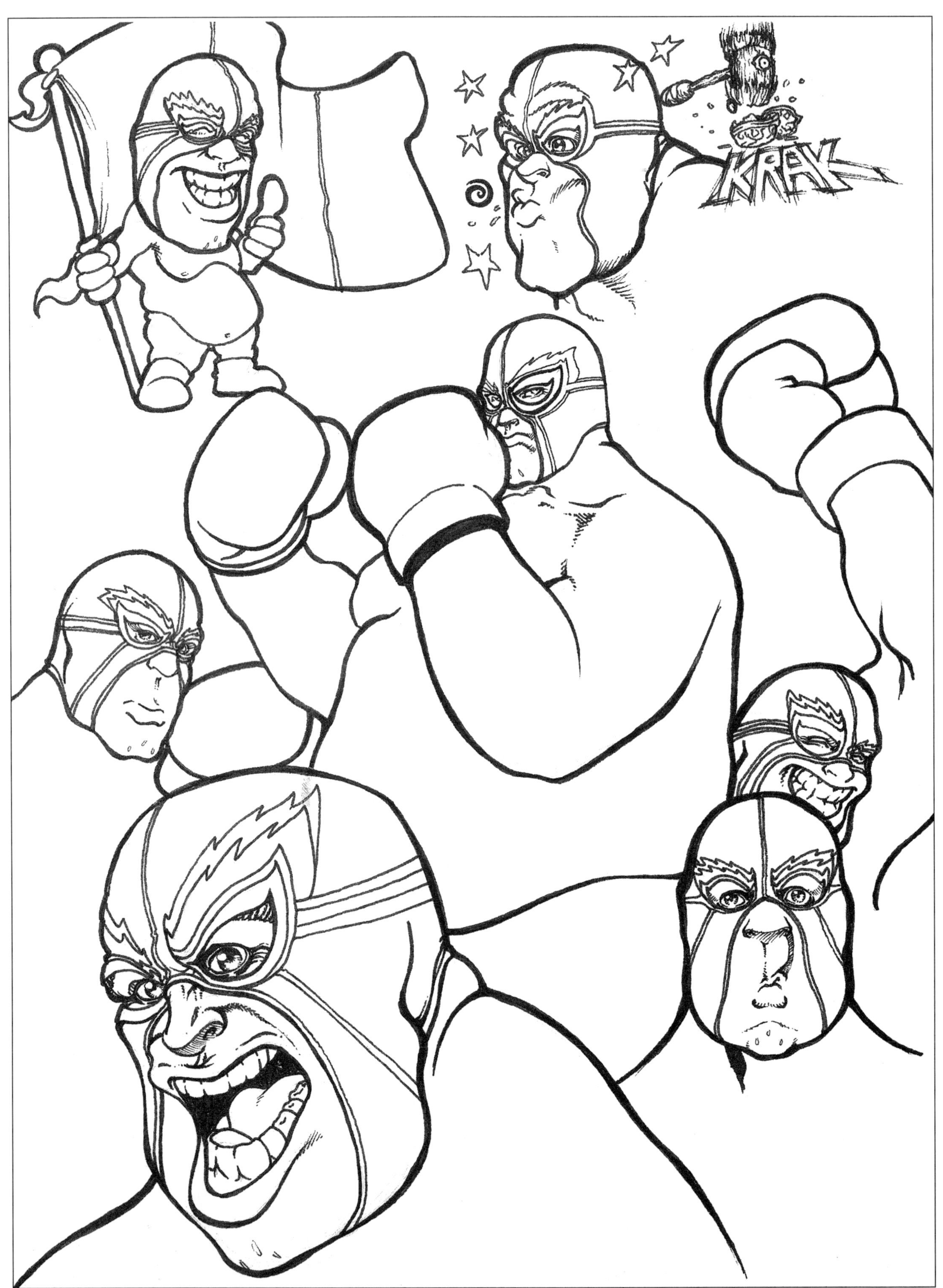
KRAK

This was a quick sketch after I saw my friend's new car with a GIANT bike rack on the back. The bike rack (The Beak) stuck out into the parking lot about half a car length, and the SUV was already HUGE.

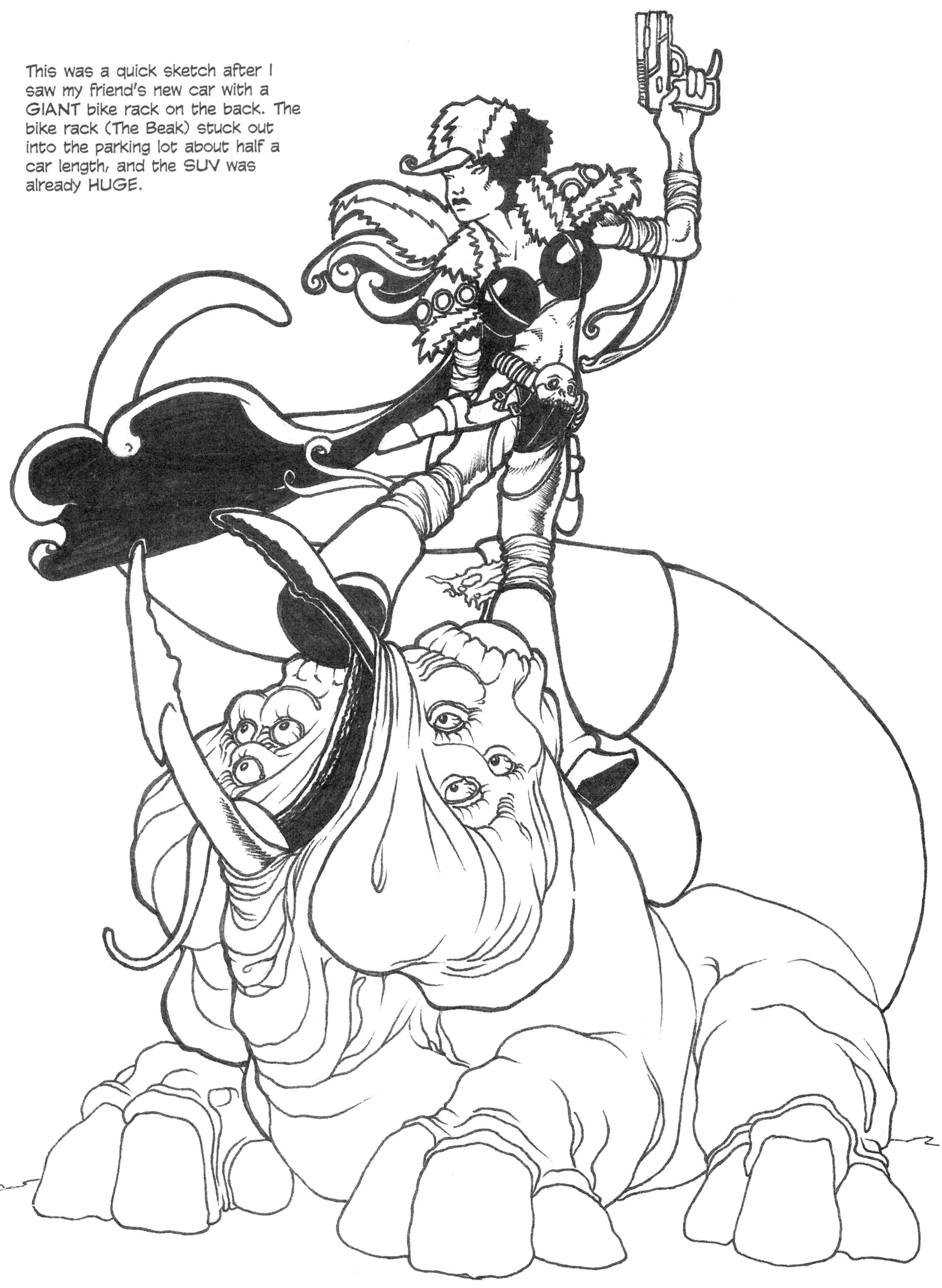

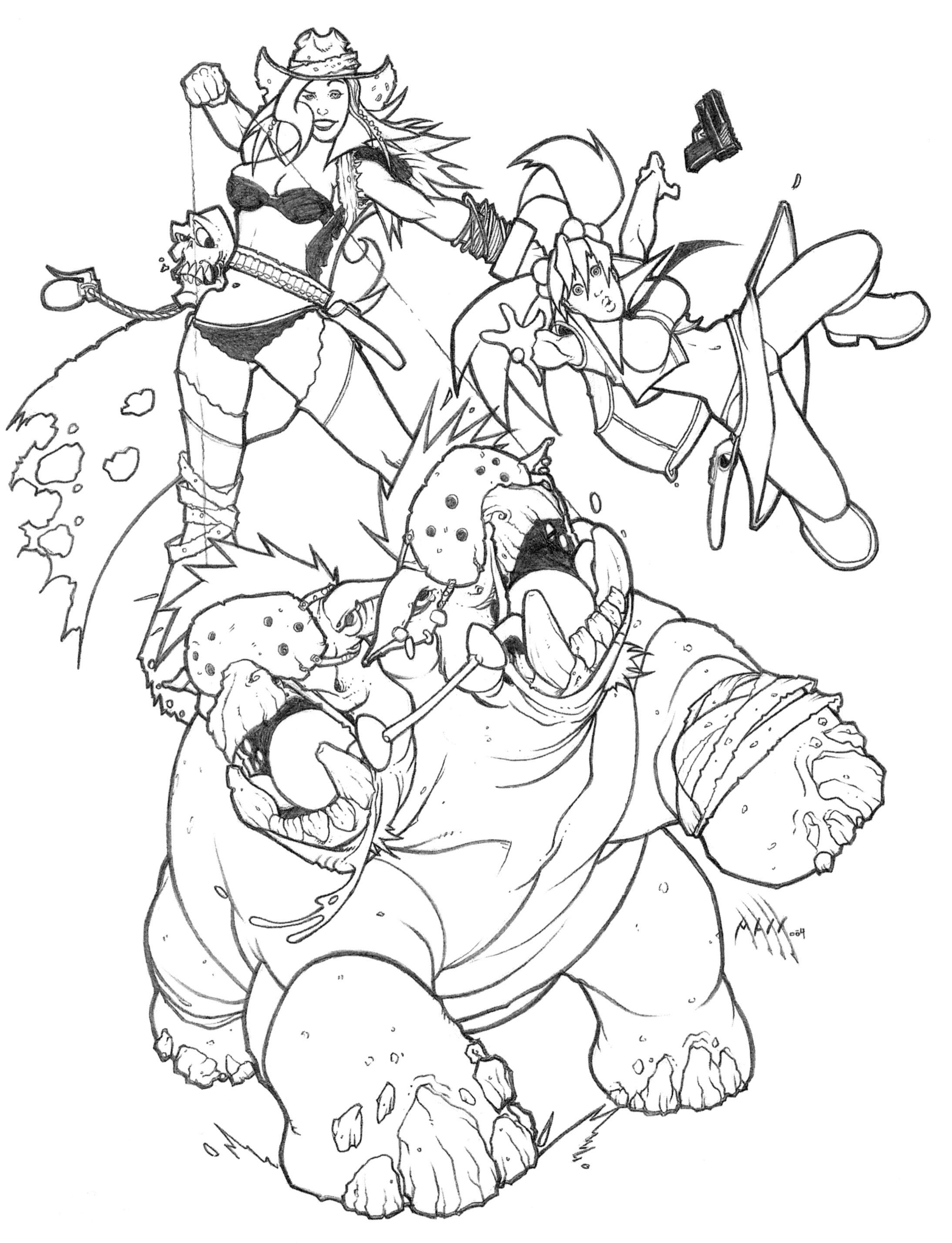
MAXX 004

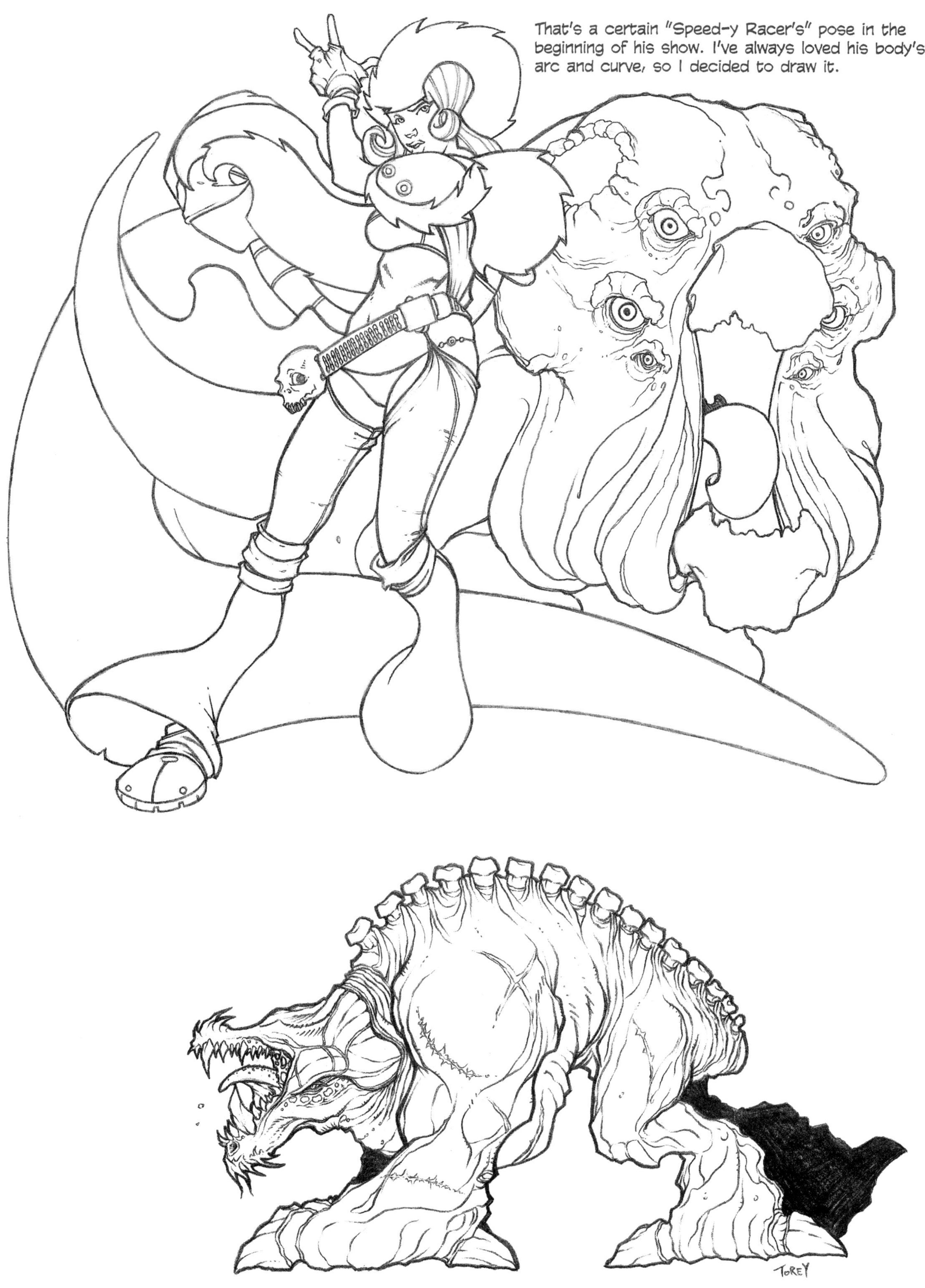
That's a certain "Speed-y Racer's" pose in the beginning of his show. I've always loved his body's arc and curve, so I decided to draw it.
TOREY

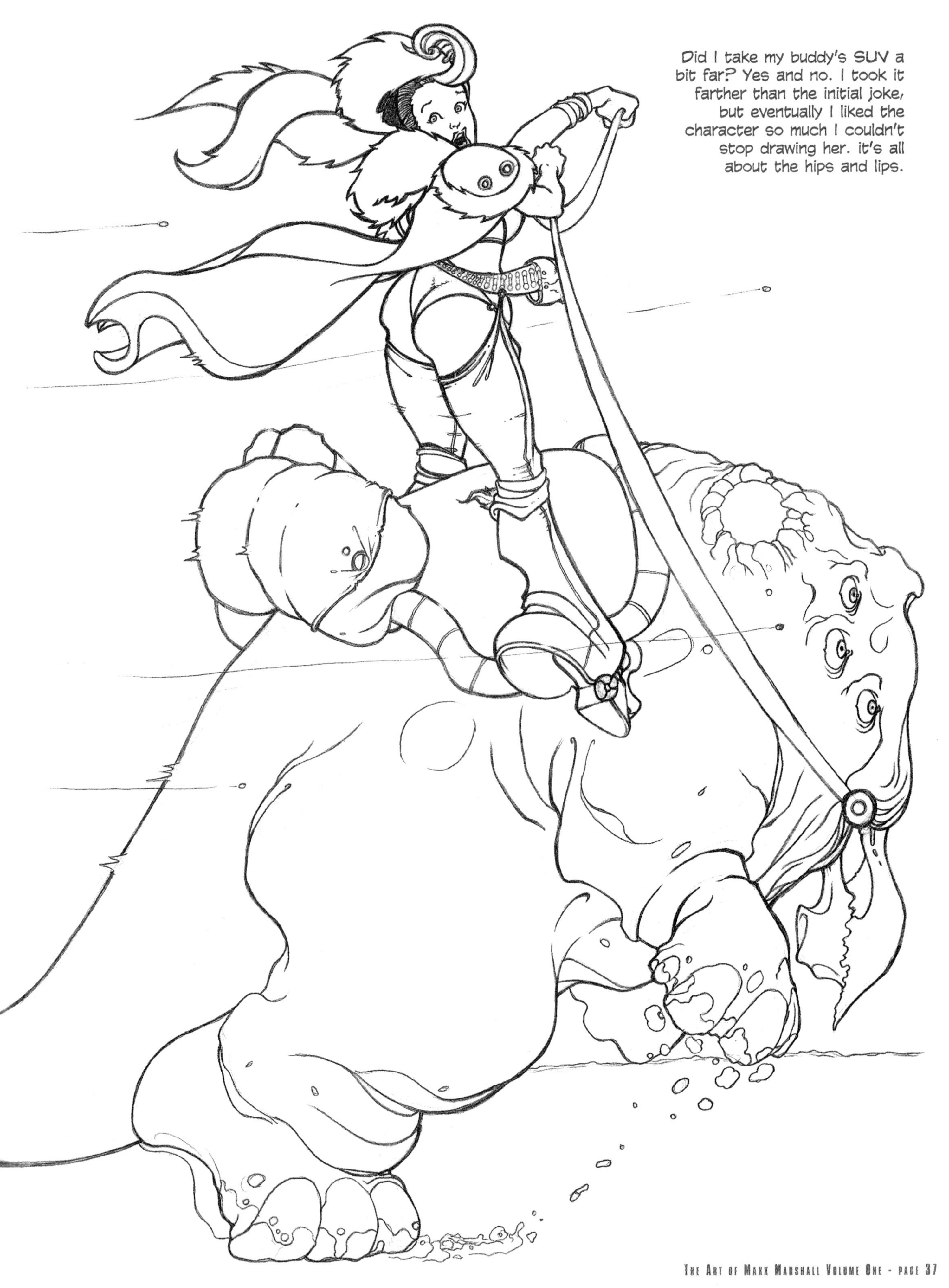

Did I take my buddy's SUV a bit far? Yes and no. I took it farther than the initial joke, but eventually I liked the character so much I couldn't stop drawing her. it's all about the hips and lips.

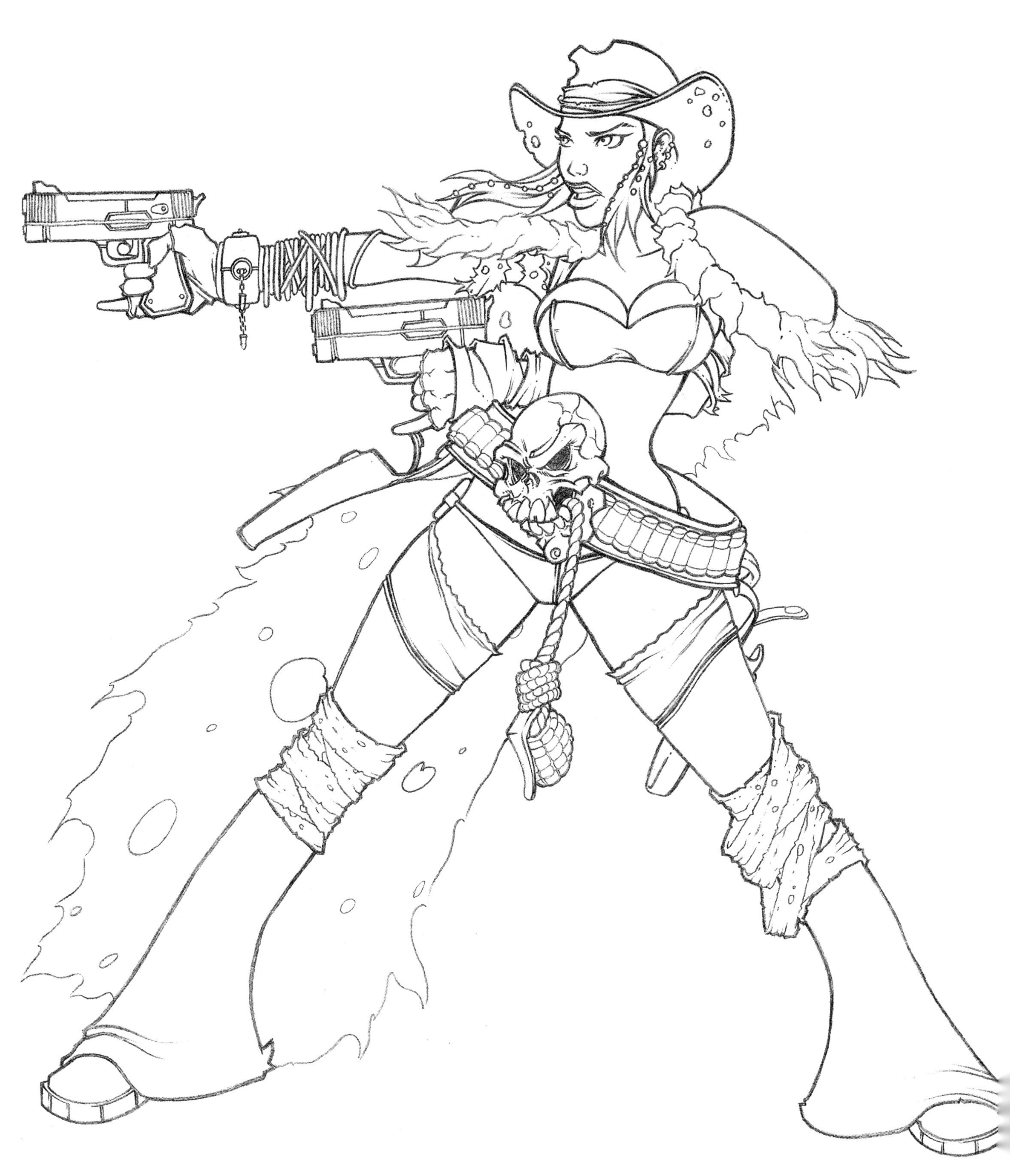

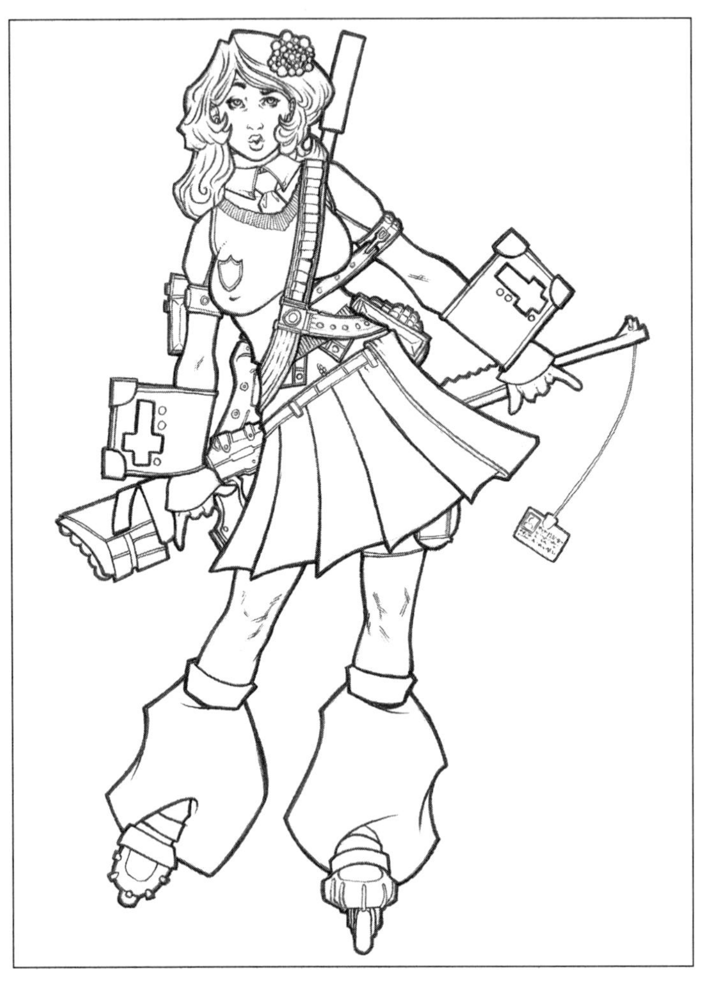
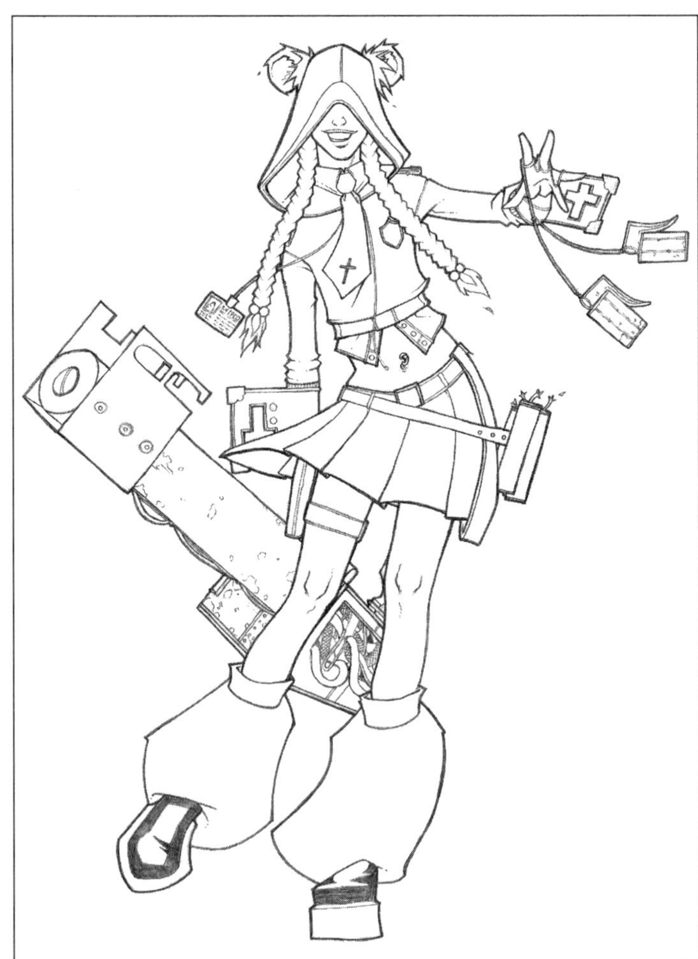
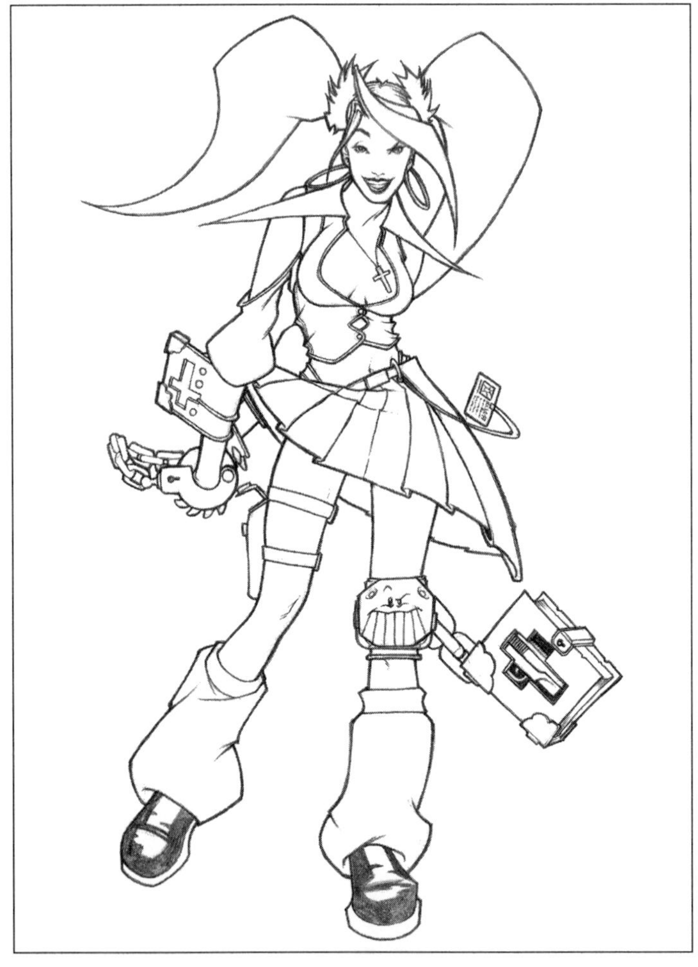
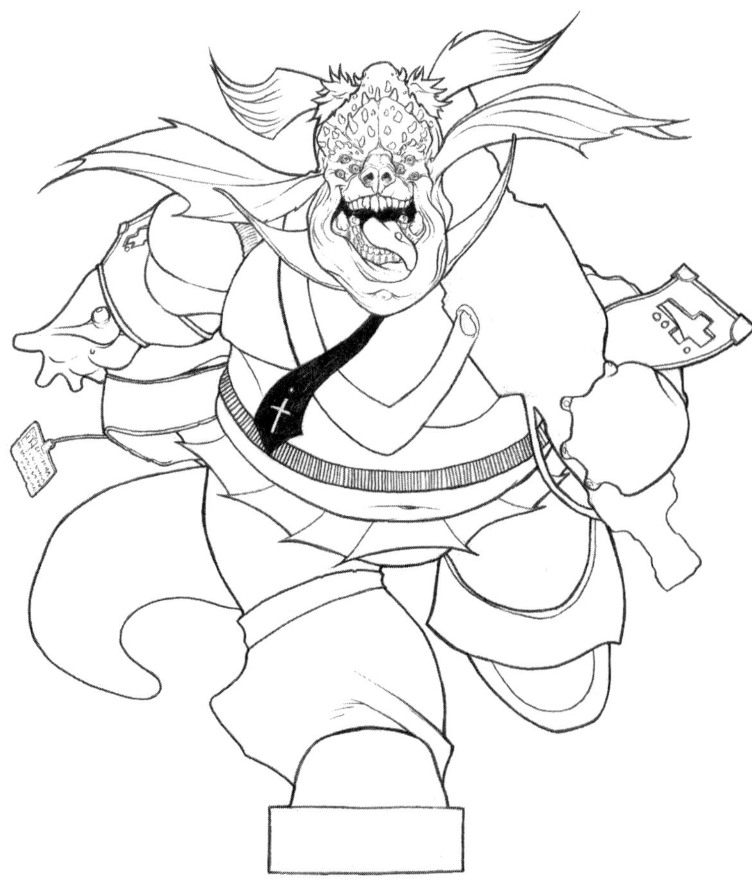

If I worked in color more, you'd be able to tell that this is a woman. But I don't, so you can't. HAHAHAHA!!!

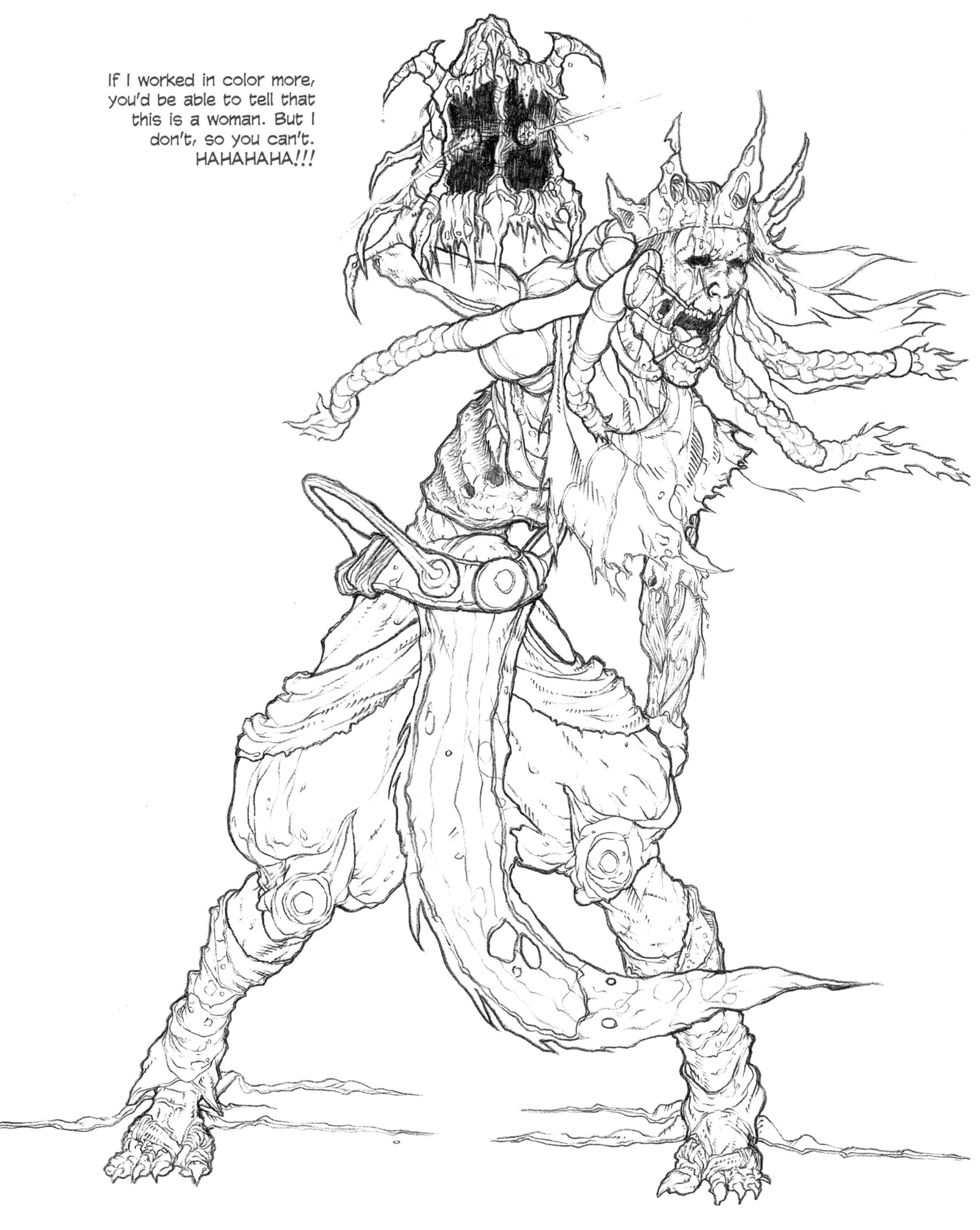

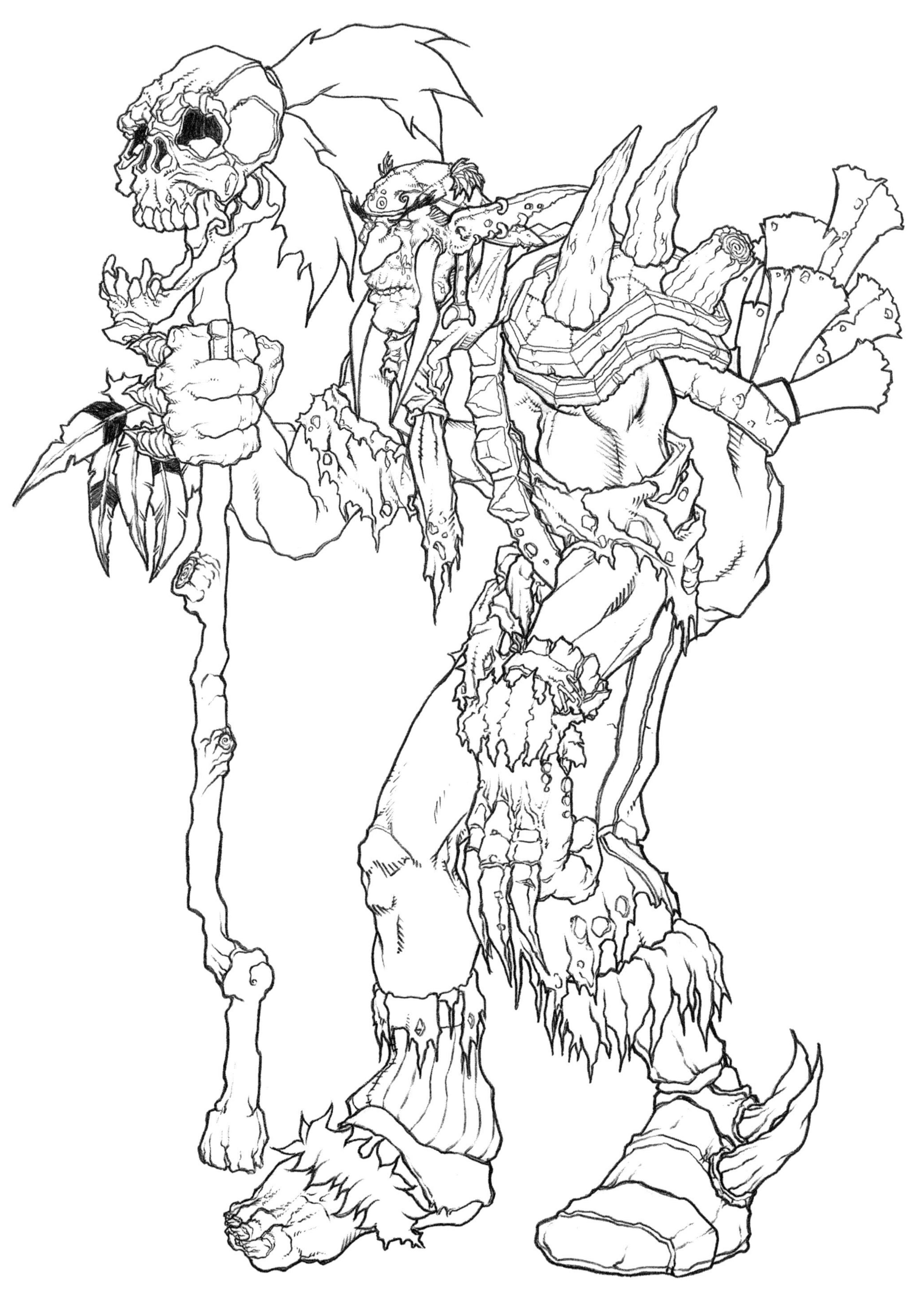

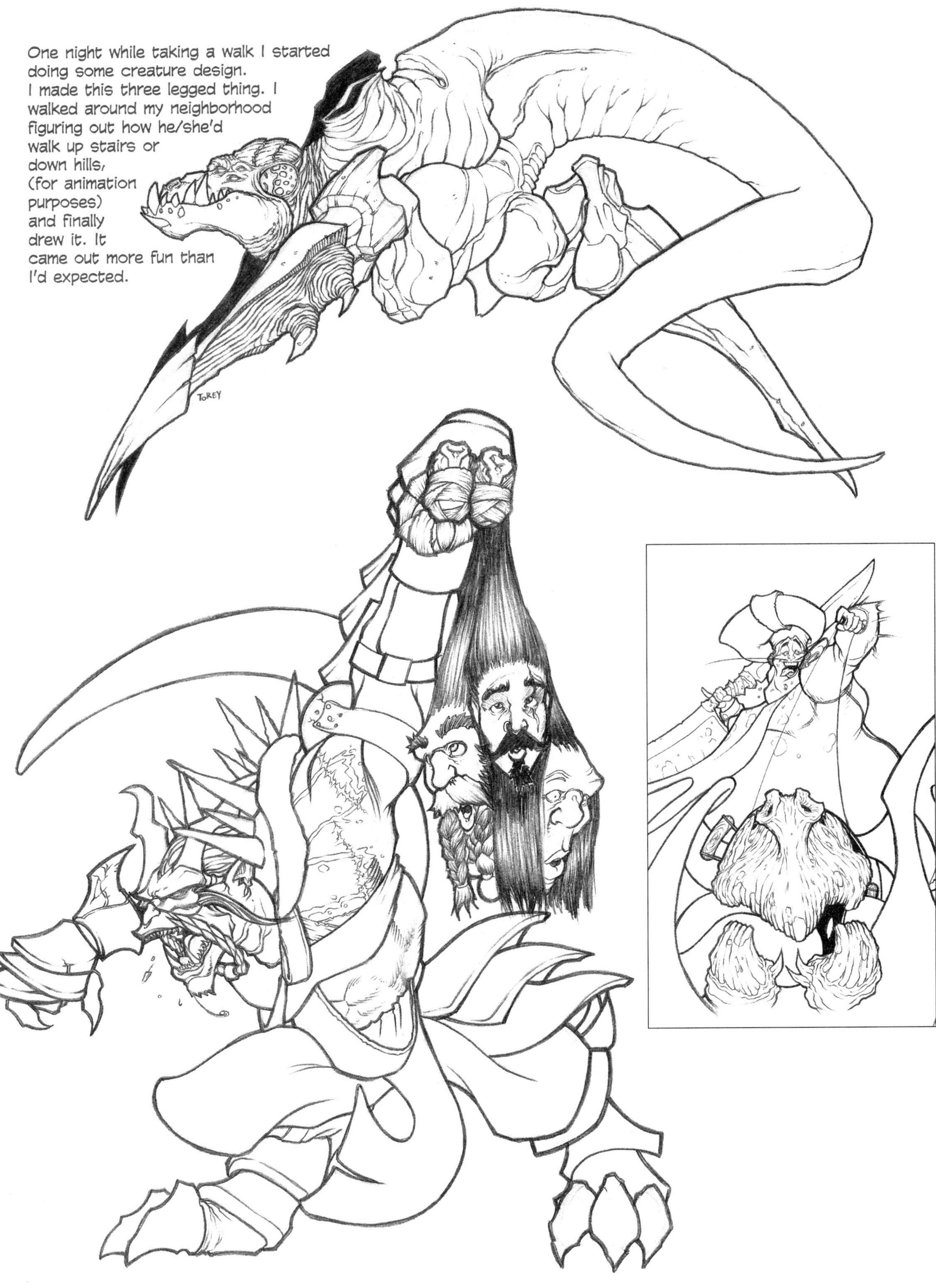

One night while taking a walk I started doing some creature design. I made this three legged thing. I walked around my neighborhood figuring out how he/she'd walk up stairs or down hills, (for animation purposes) and finally drew it. It came out more fun than I'd expected.

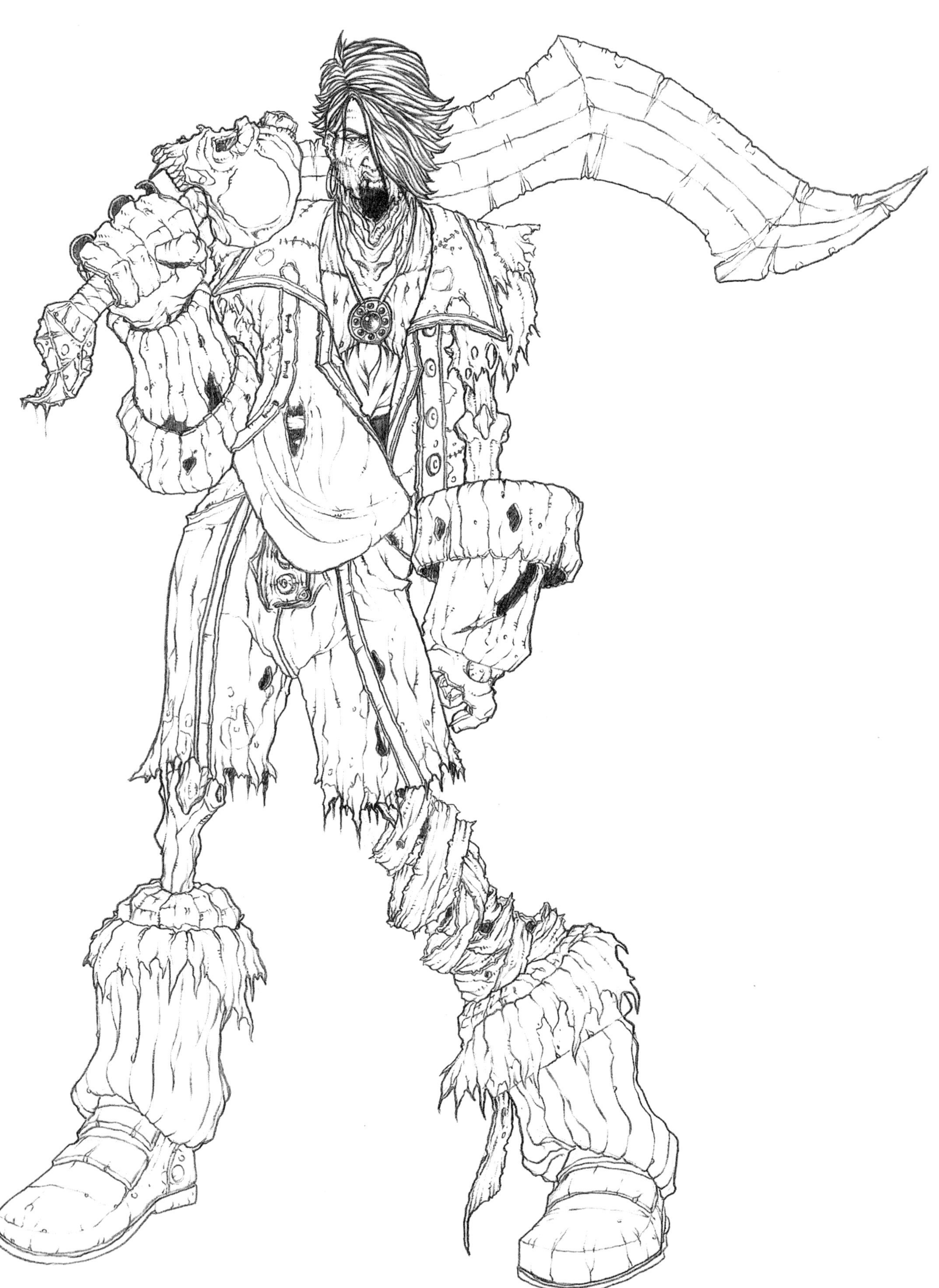

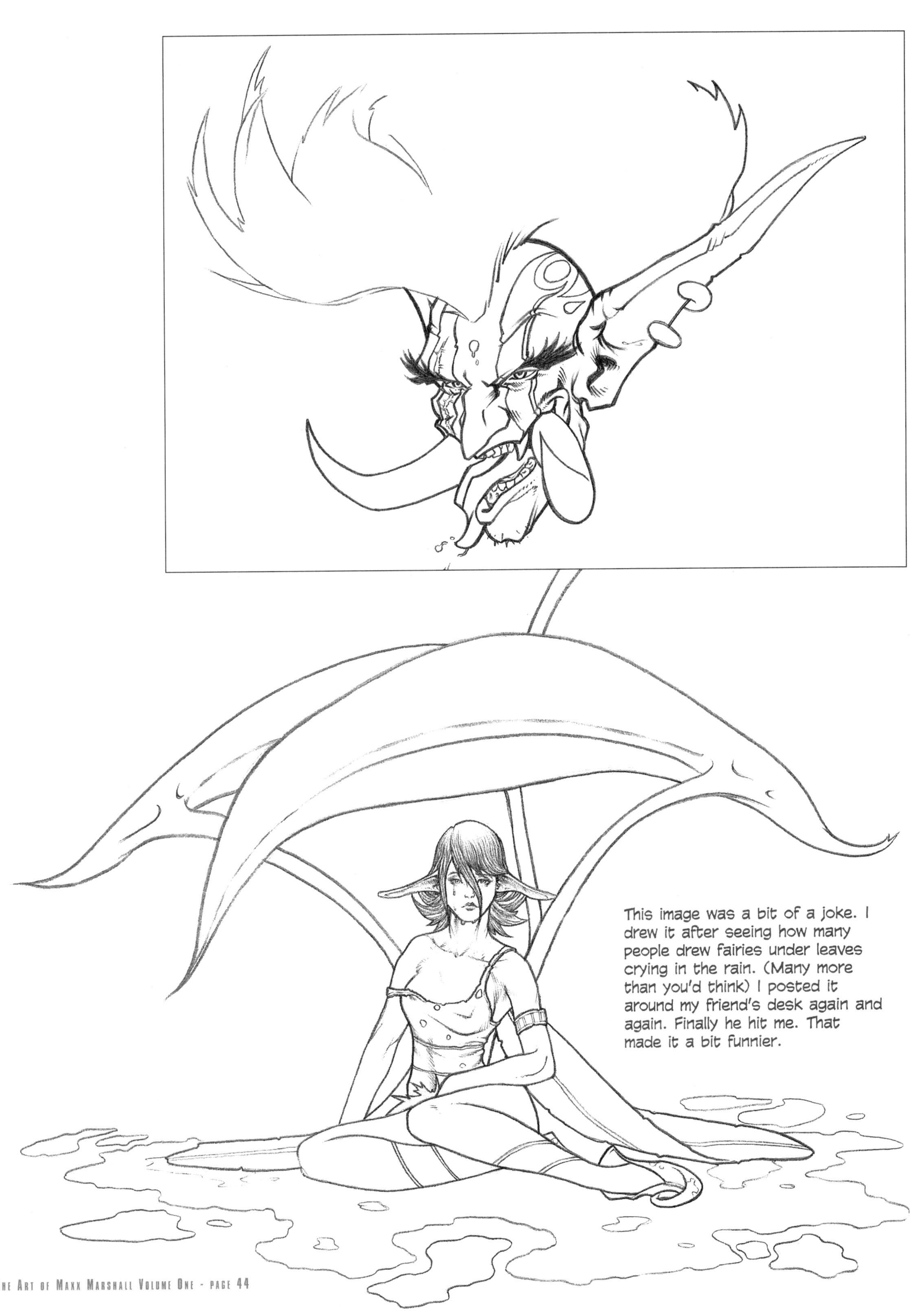

This image was a bit of a joke. I drew it after seeing how many people drew fairies under leaves crying in the rain. (Many more than you'd think) I posted it around my friend's desk again and again. Finally he hit me. That made it a bit funnier.

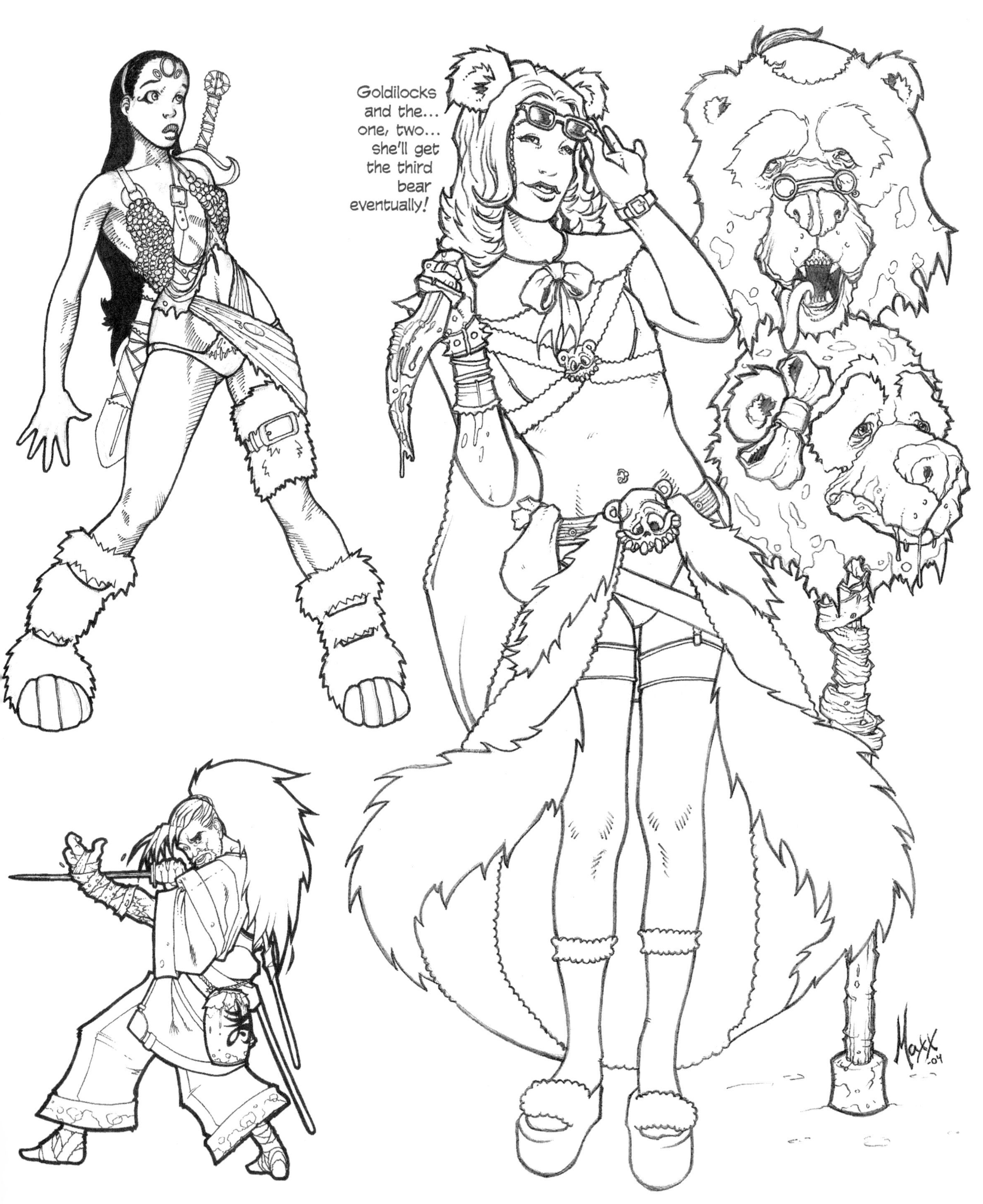
Goldilocks
and the...
one, two...
she'll get
the third
bear
eventually!
Maxx '04

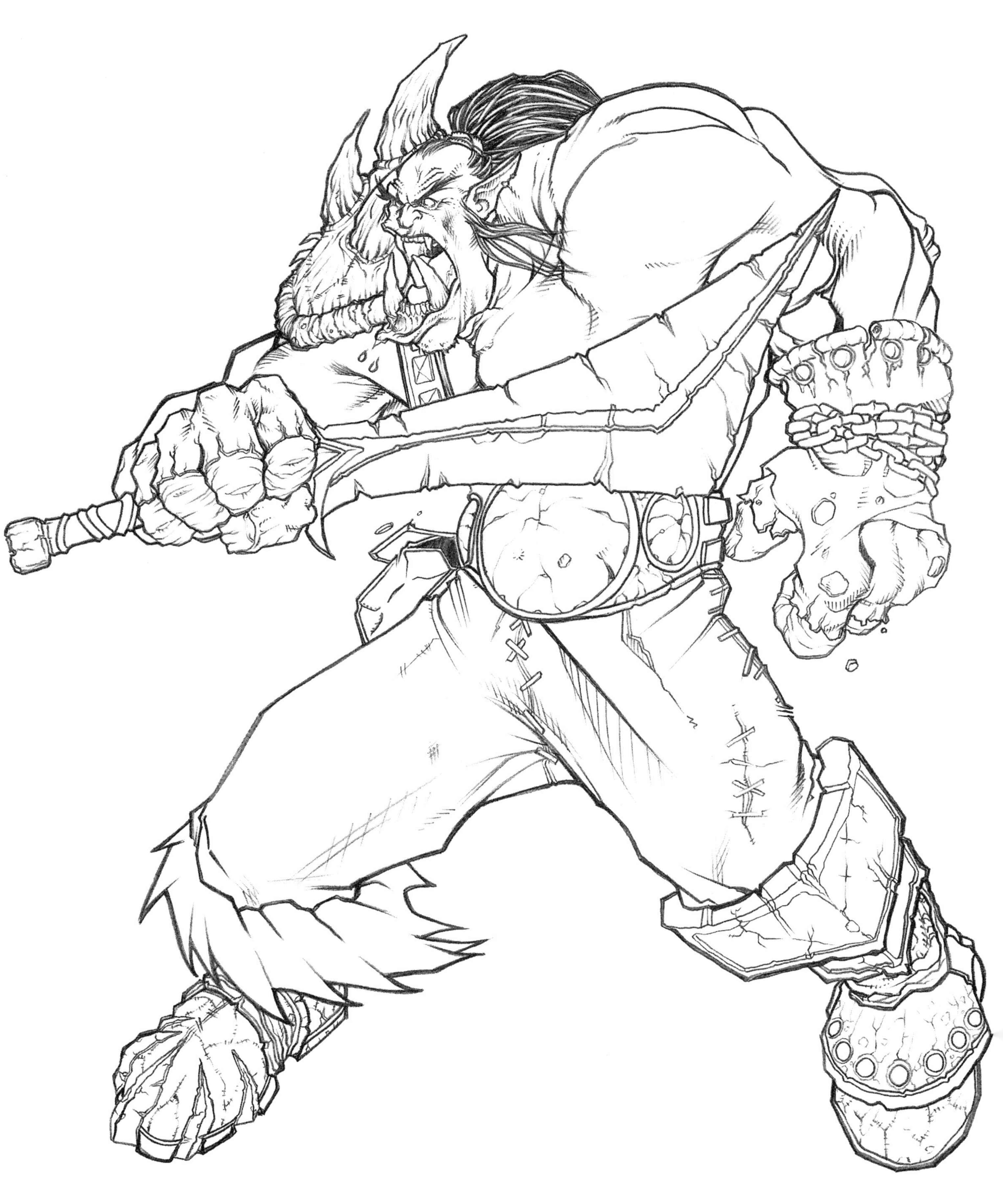

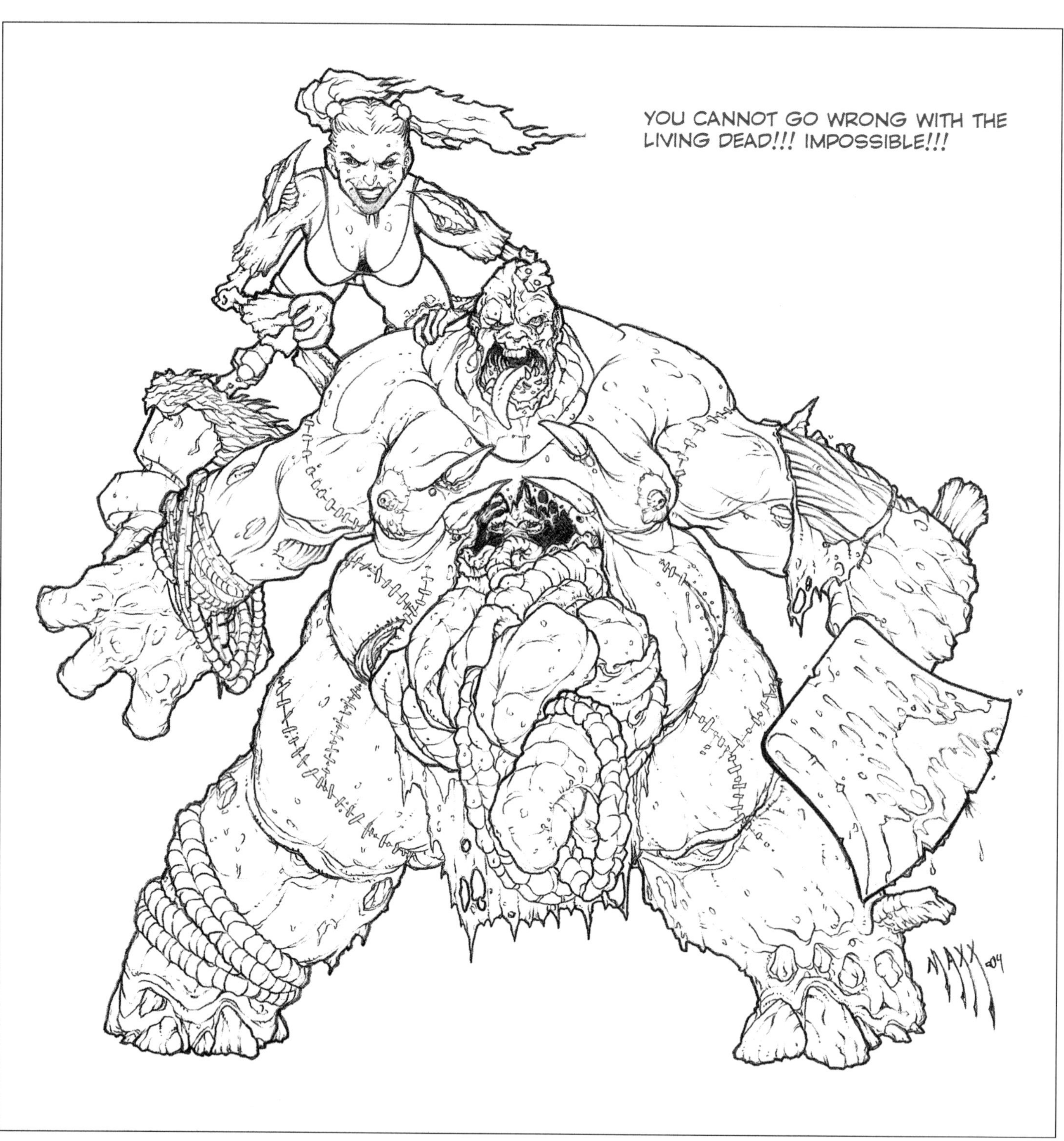
YOU CANNOT GO WRONG WITH THE
LIVING DEAD!!! IMPOSSIBLE!!!
MAXX '04

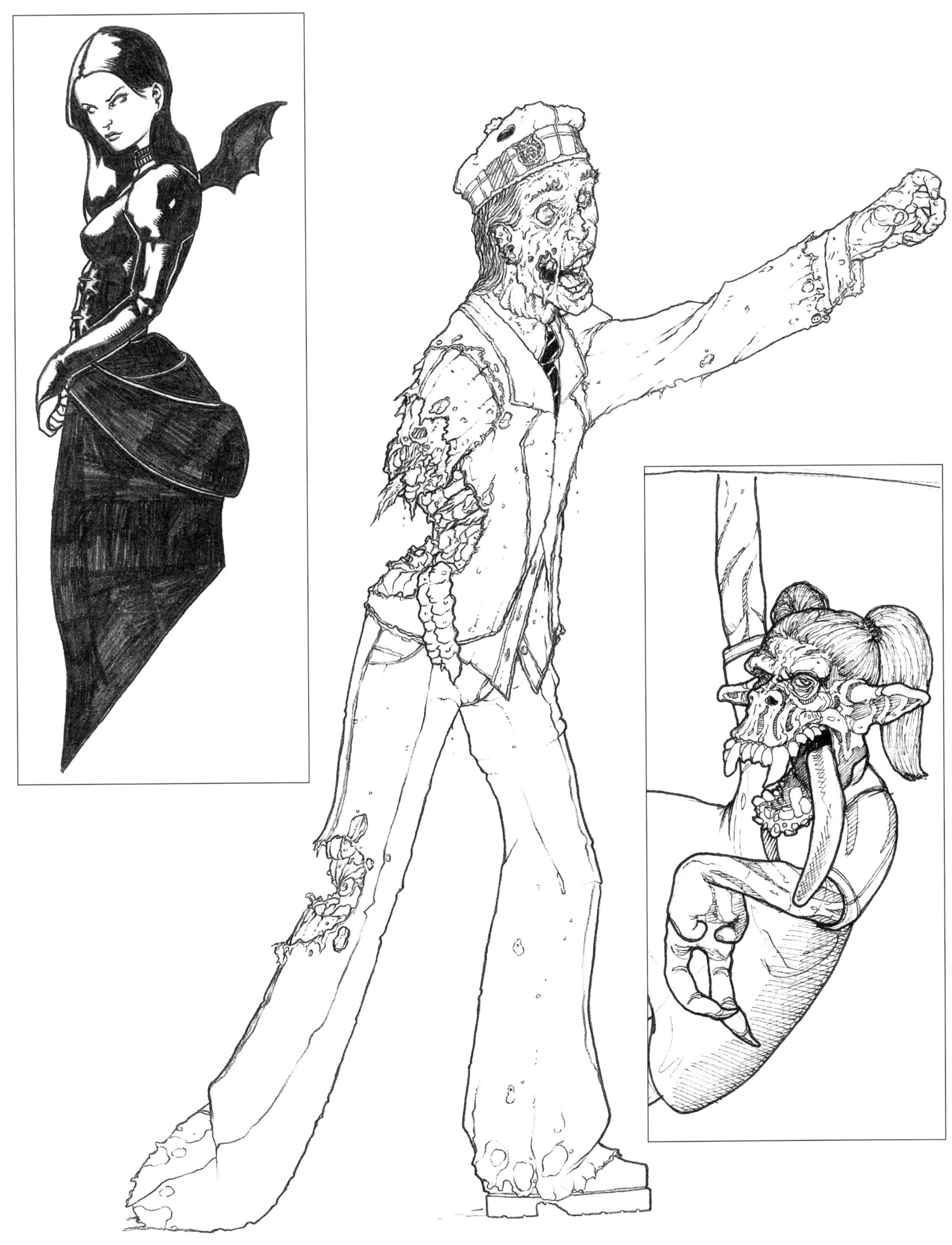

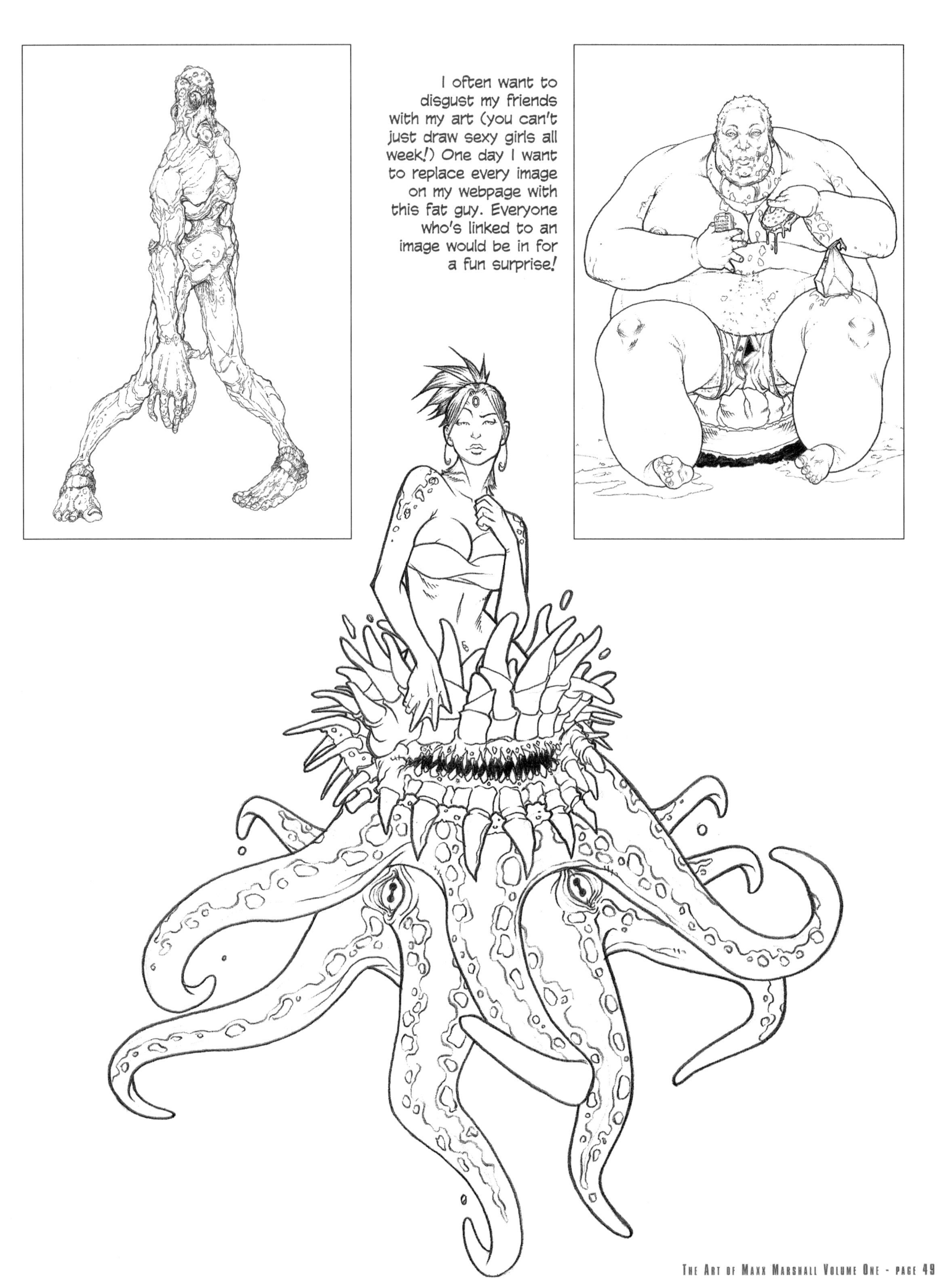

I often want to disgust my friends with my art (you can't just draw sexy girls all week!) One day I want to replace every image on my webpage with this fat guy. Everyone who's linked to an image would be in for a fun surprise!

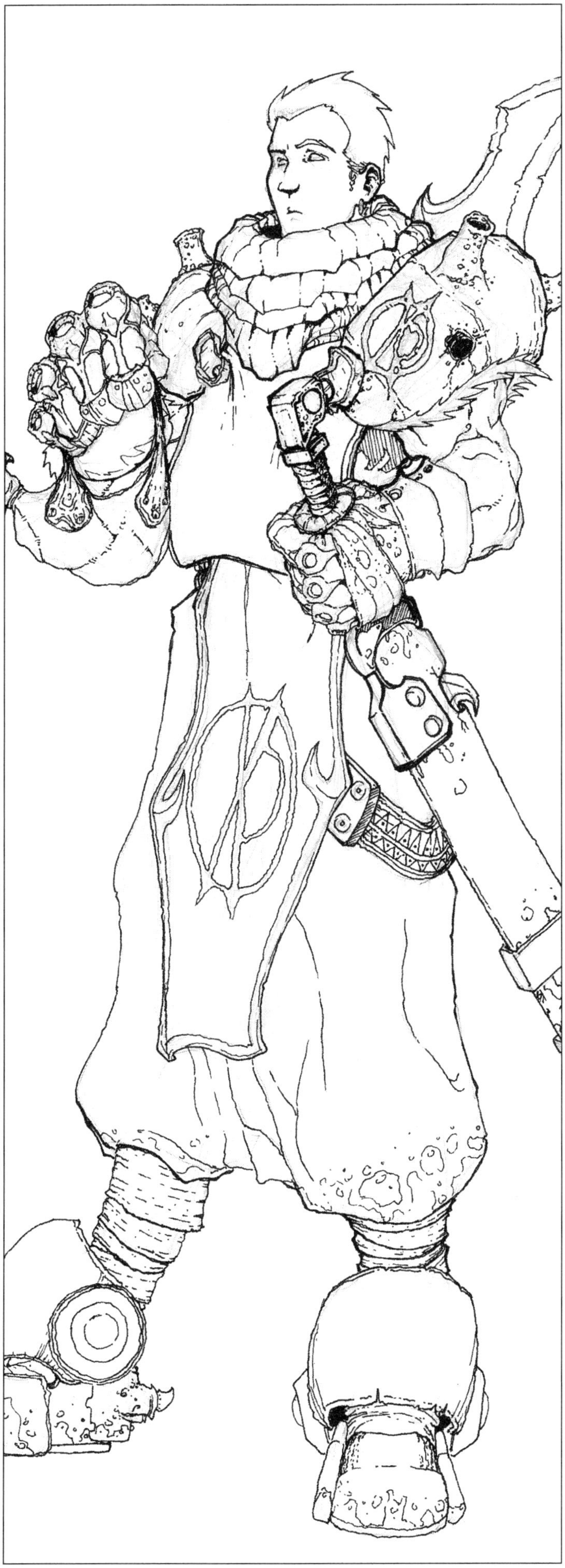

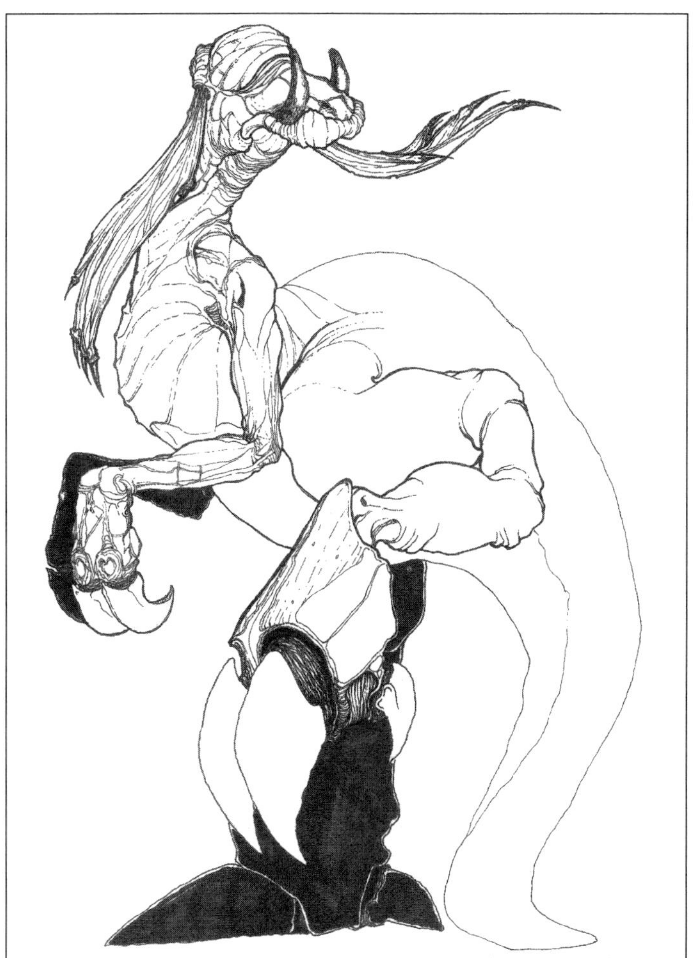

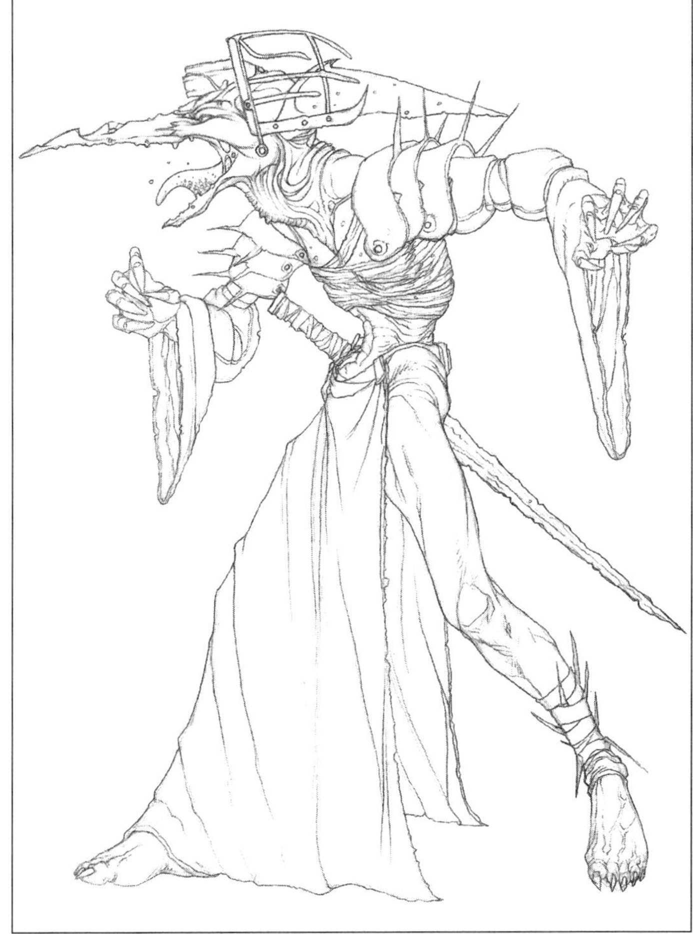

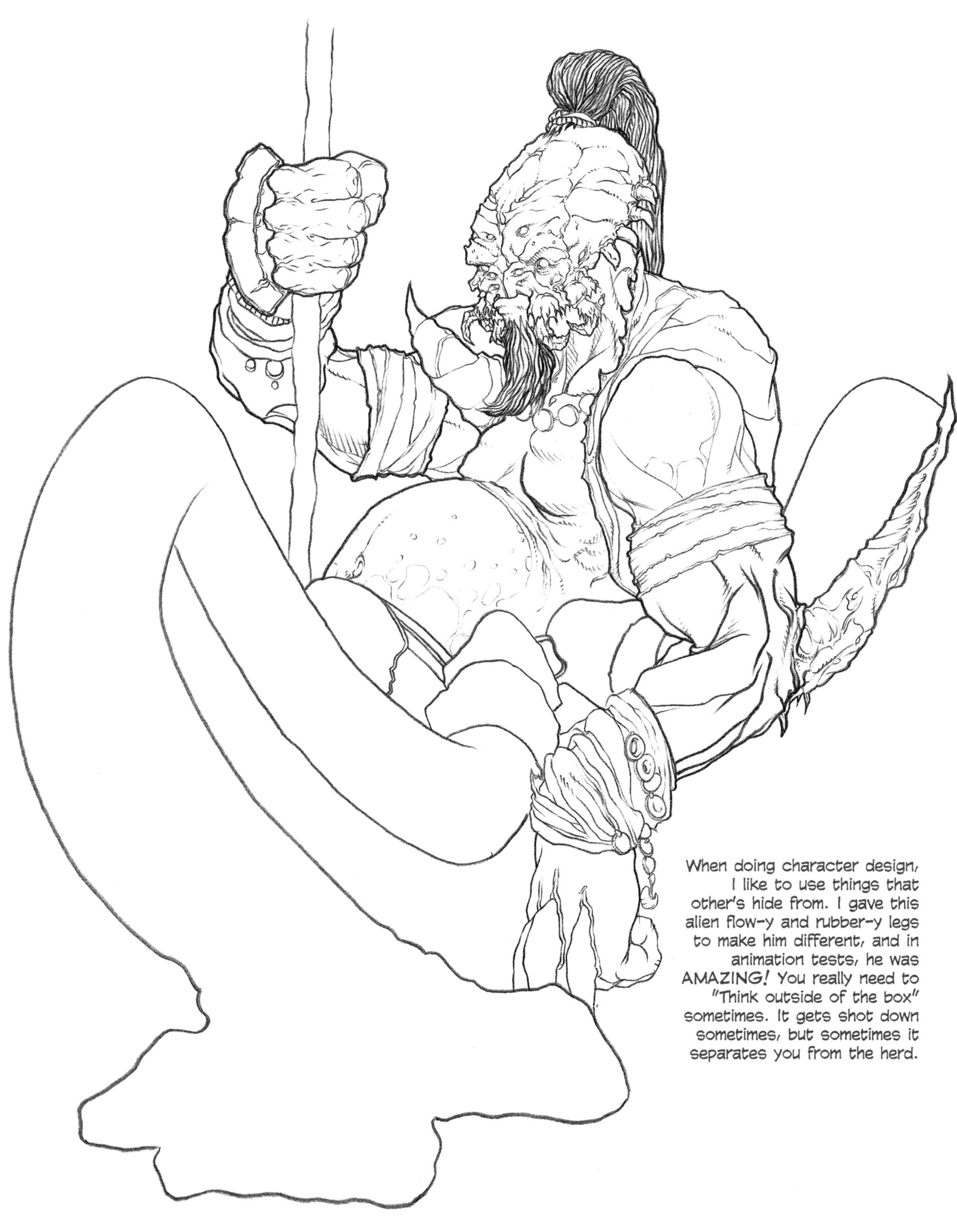

When doing character design, I like to use things that other's hide from. I gave this alien flow-y and rubber-y legs to make him different, and in animation tests, he was AMAZING! You really need to "Think outside of the box" sometimes. It gets shot down sometimes, but sometimes it separates you from the herd.

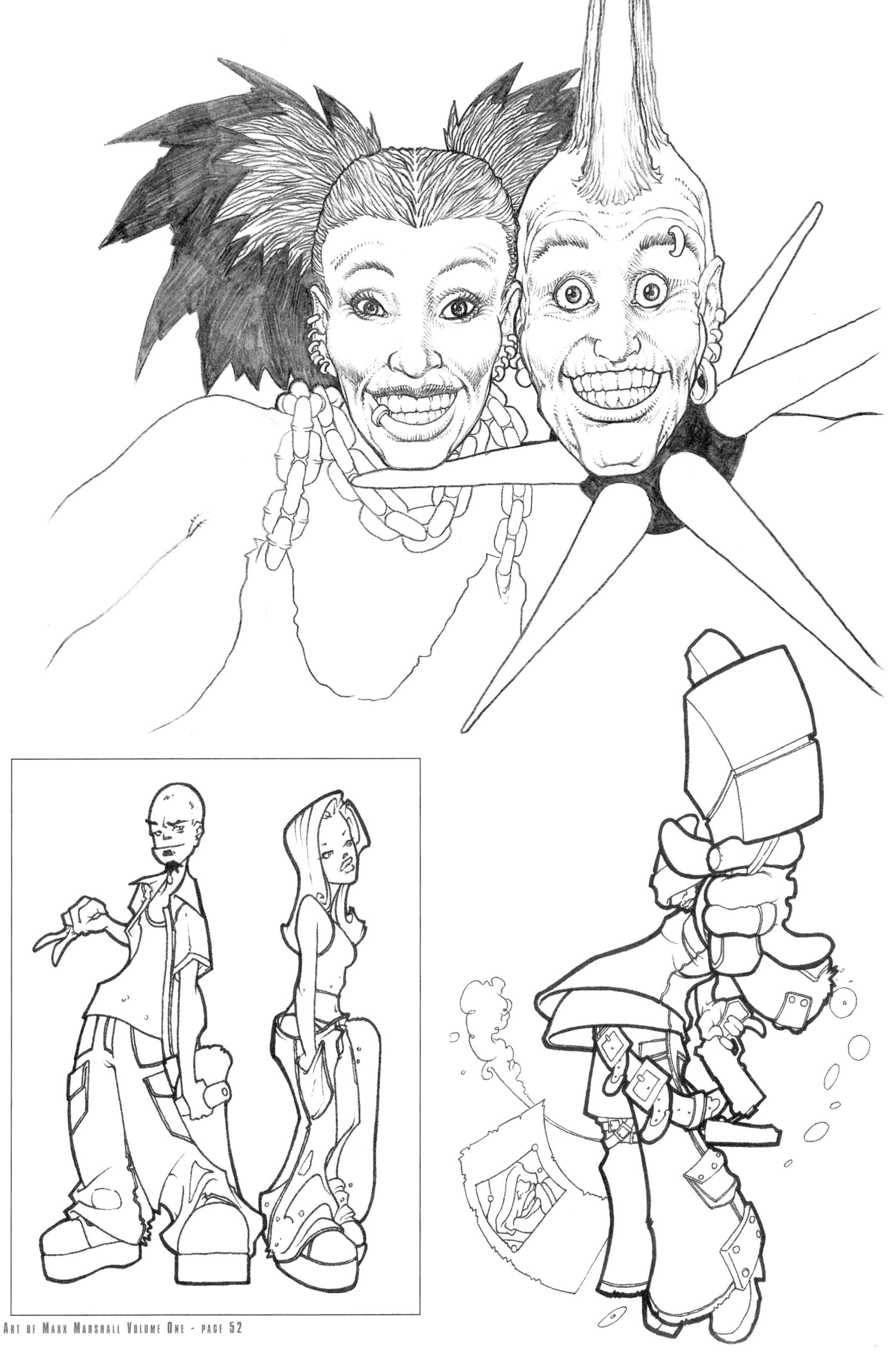

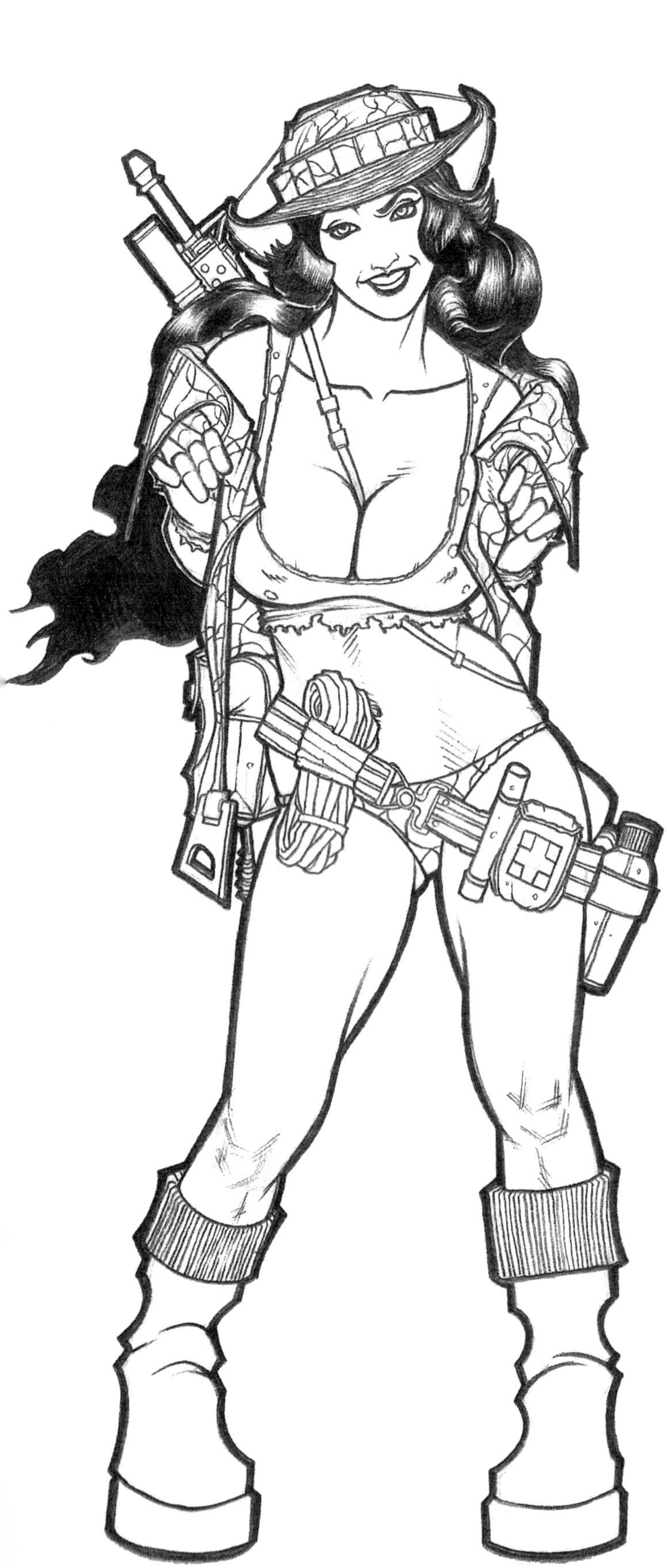

I drew this for a friend of mine.
"Her chest is too big!" came the reply
...I've never had that problem...

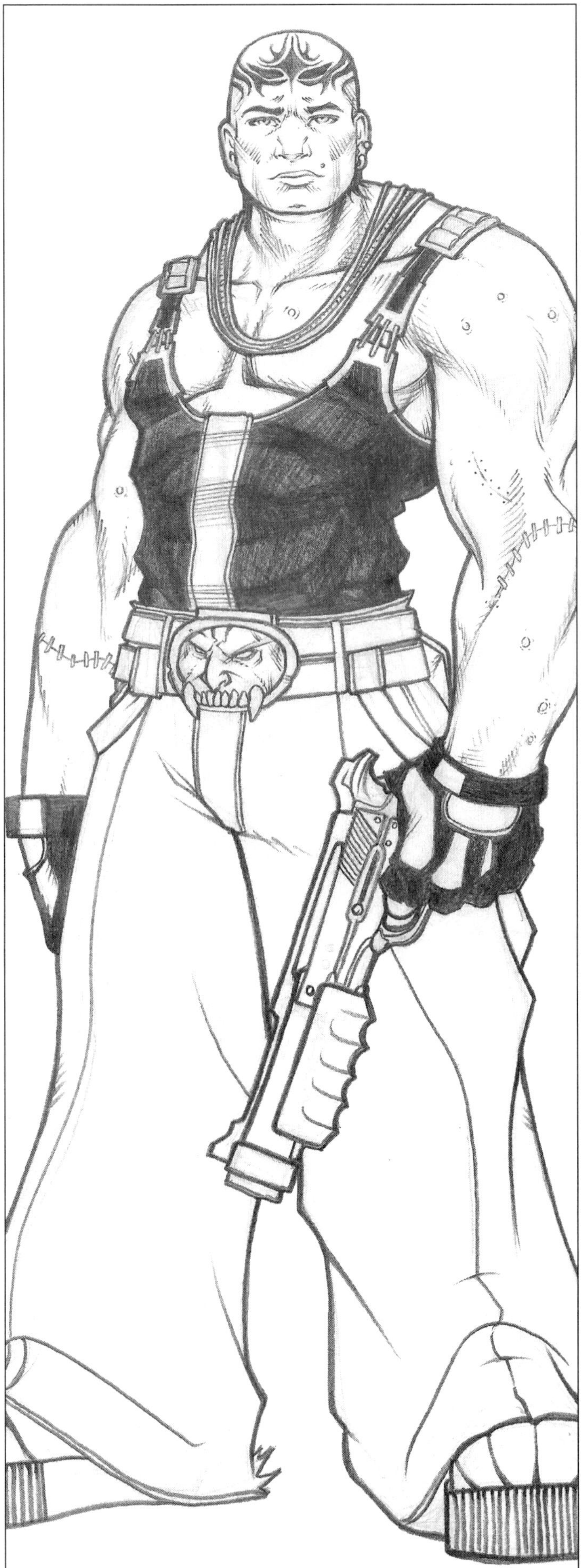

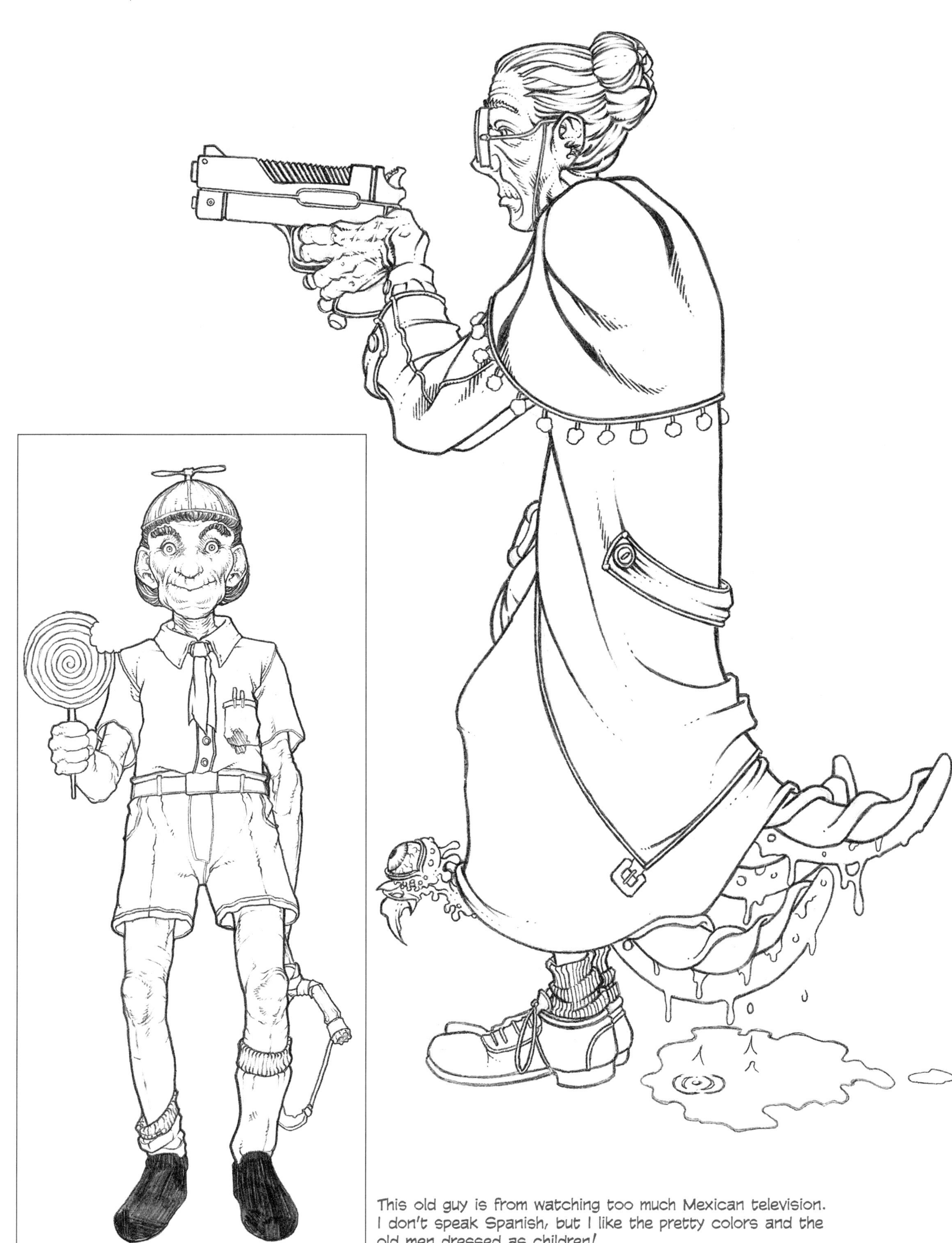

This old guy is from watching too much Mexican television. I don't speak Spanish, but I like the pretty colors and the old men dressed as children!

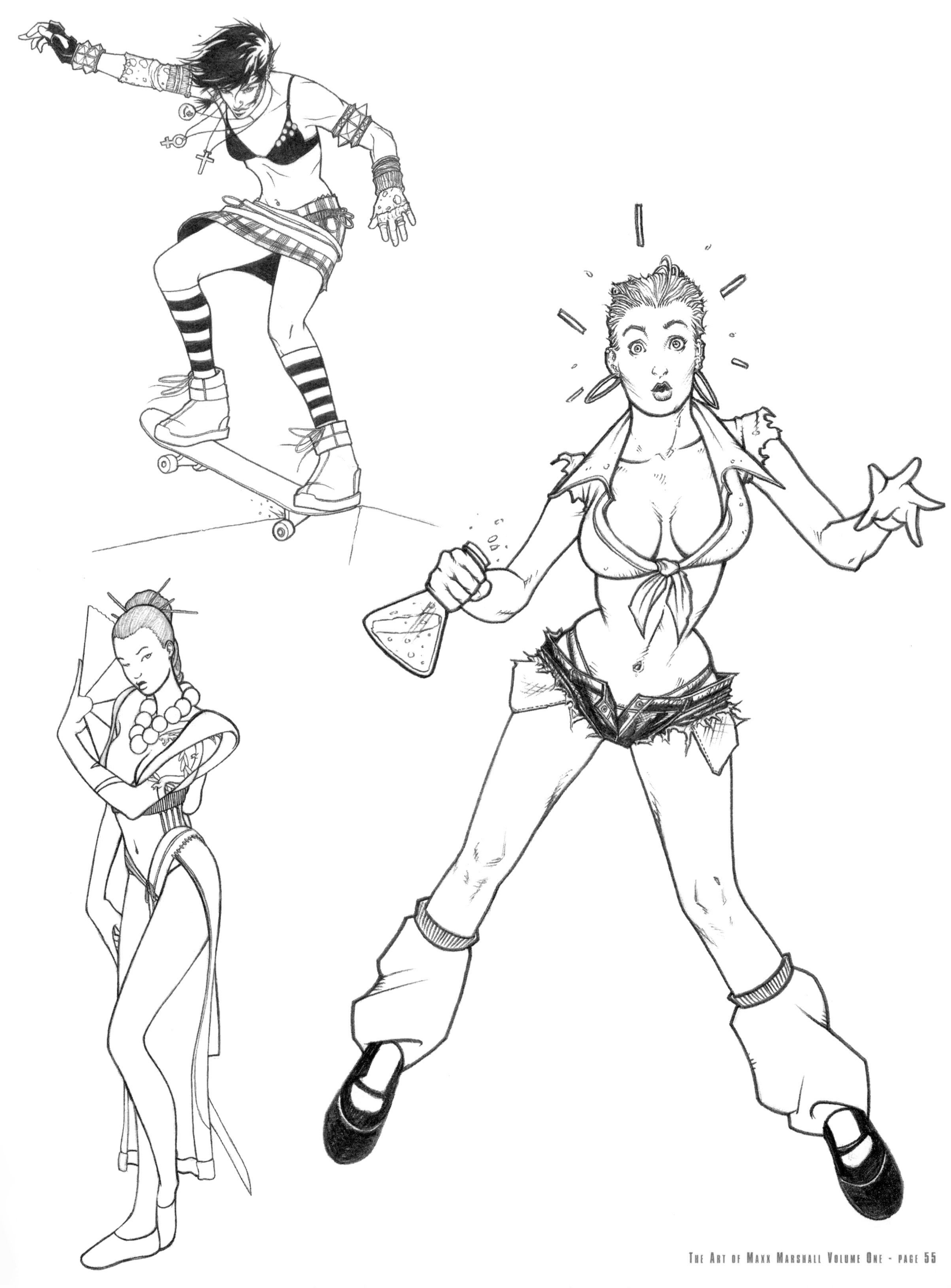

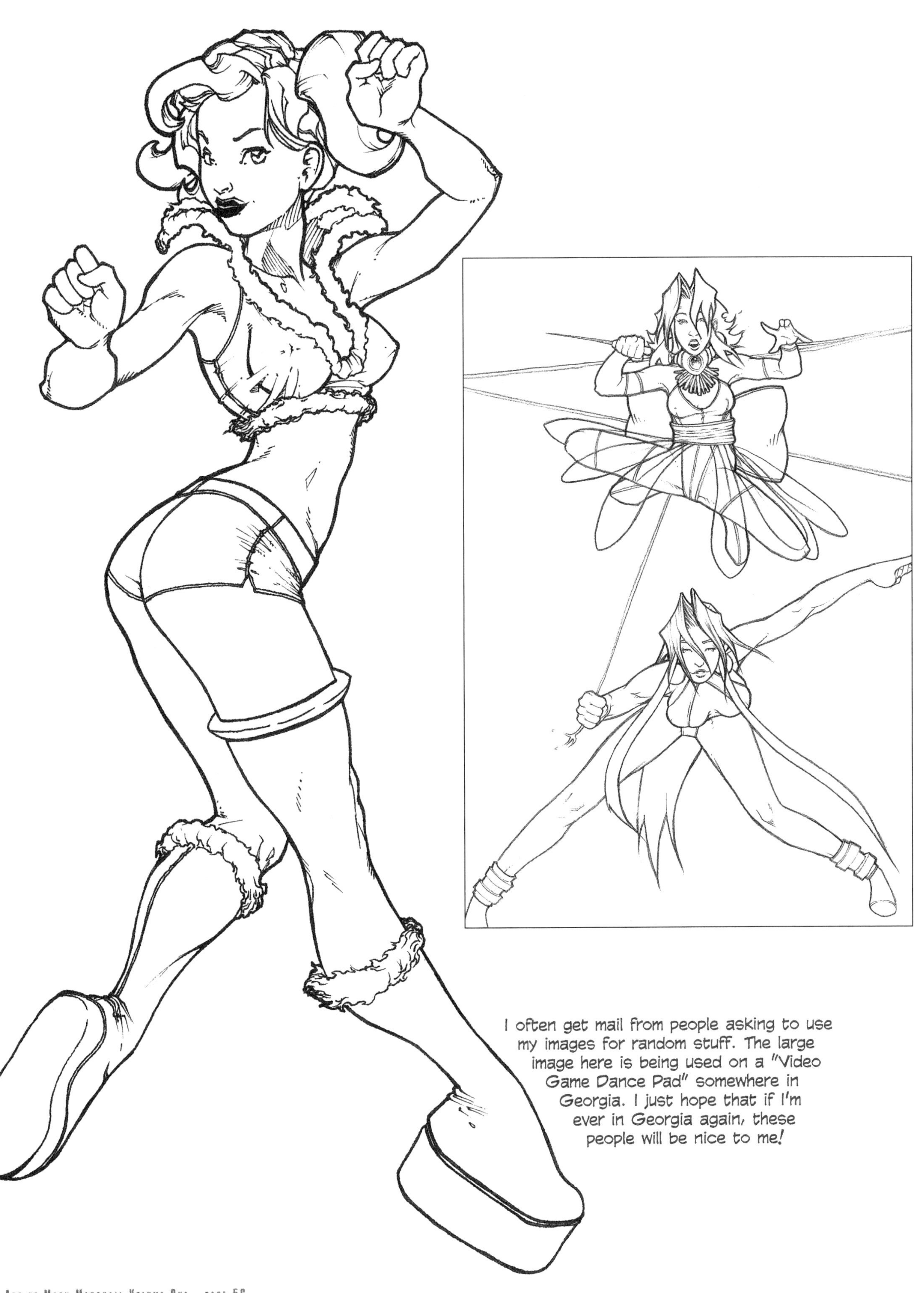

I often get mail from people asking to use my images for random stuff. The large image here is being used on a "Video Game Dance Pad" somewhere in Georgia. I just hope that if I'm ever in Georgia again, these people will be nice to me!

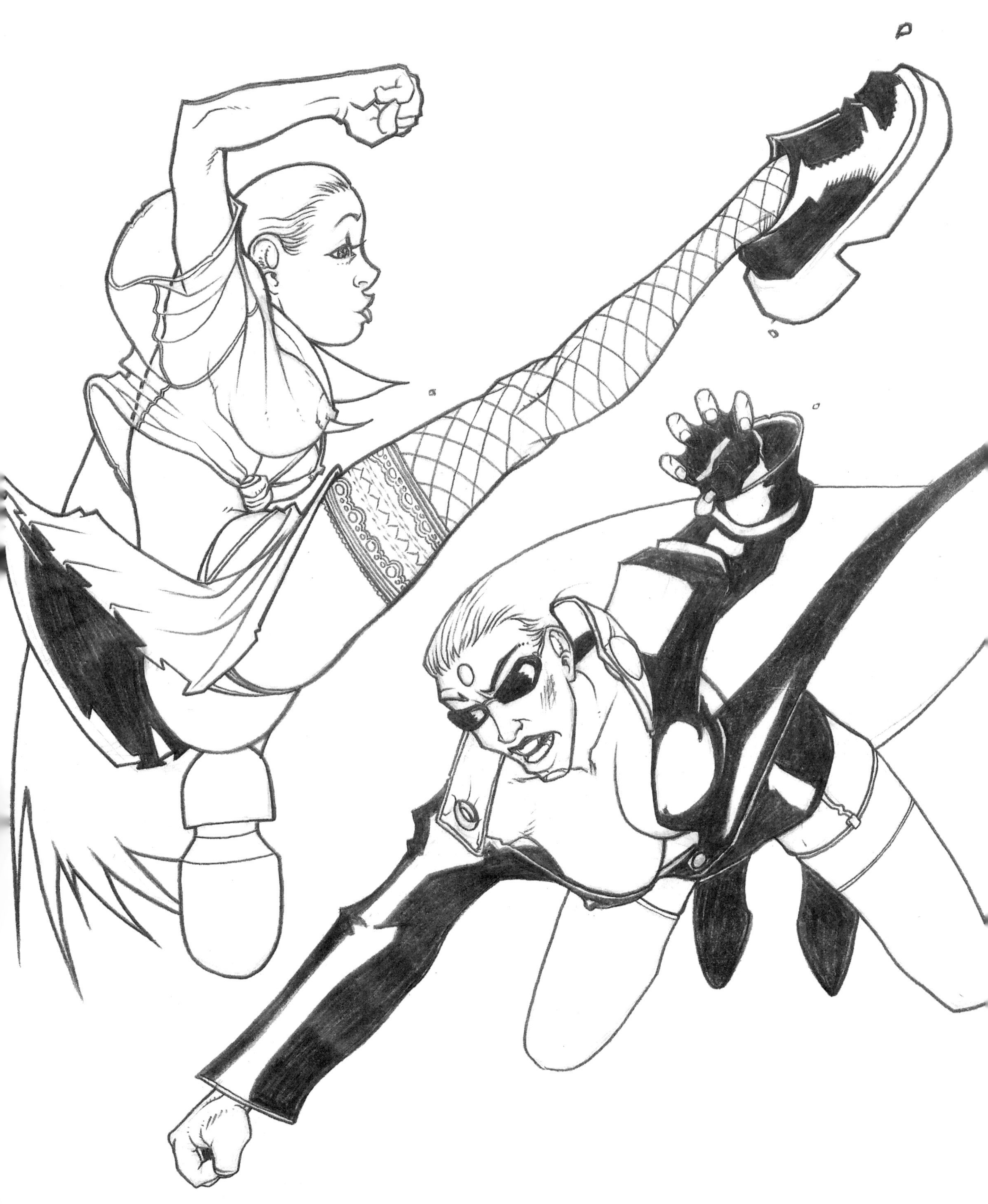

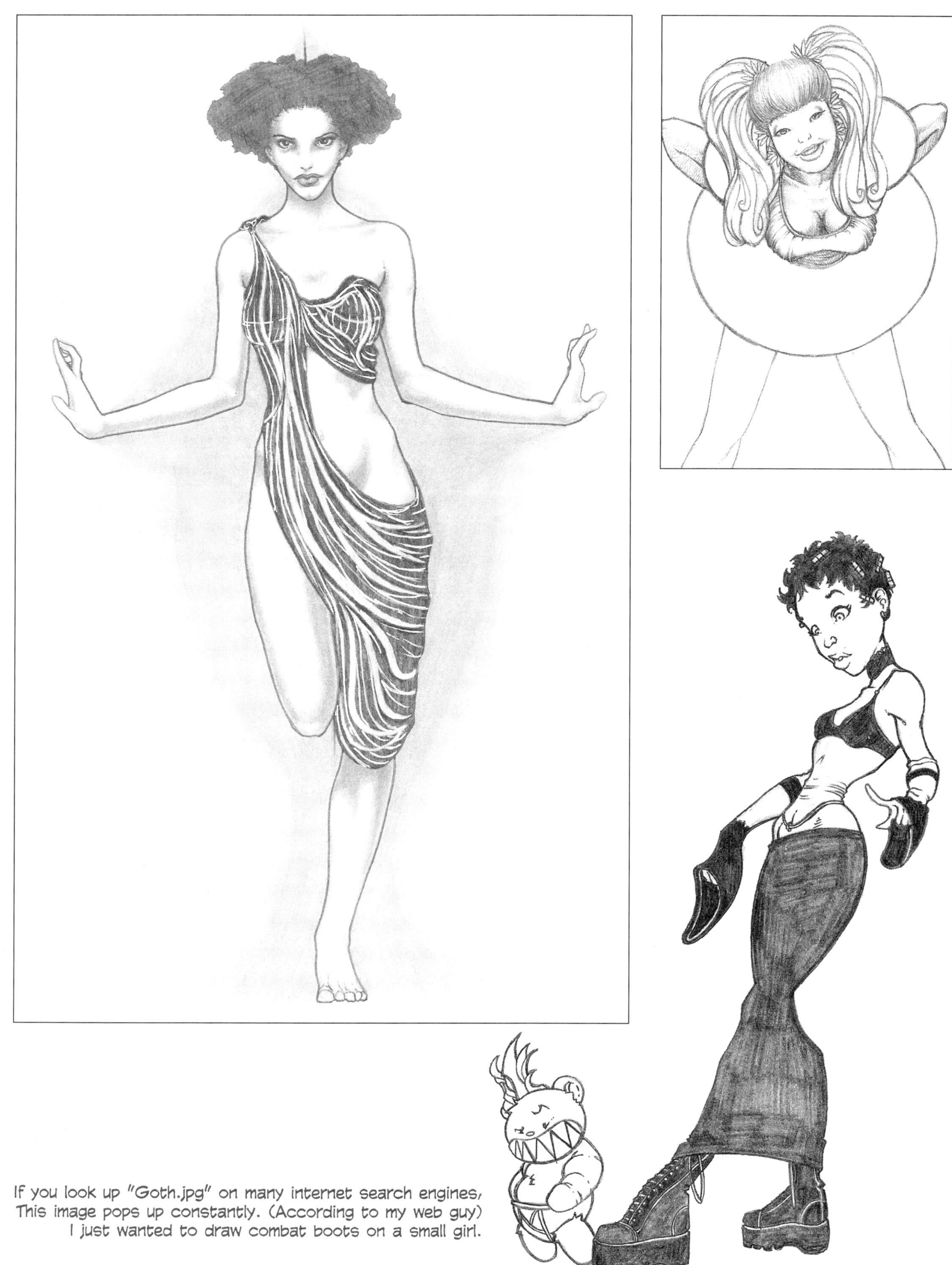

If you look up "Goth.jpg" on many internet search engines,
This image pops up constantly. (According to my web guy)
I just wanted to draw combat boots on a small girl.

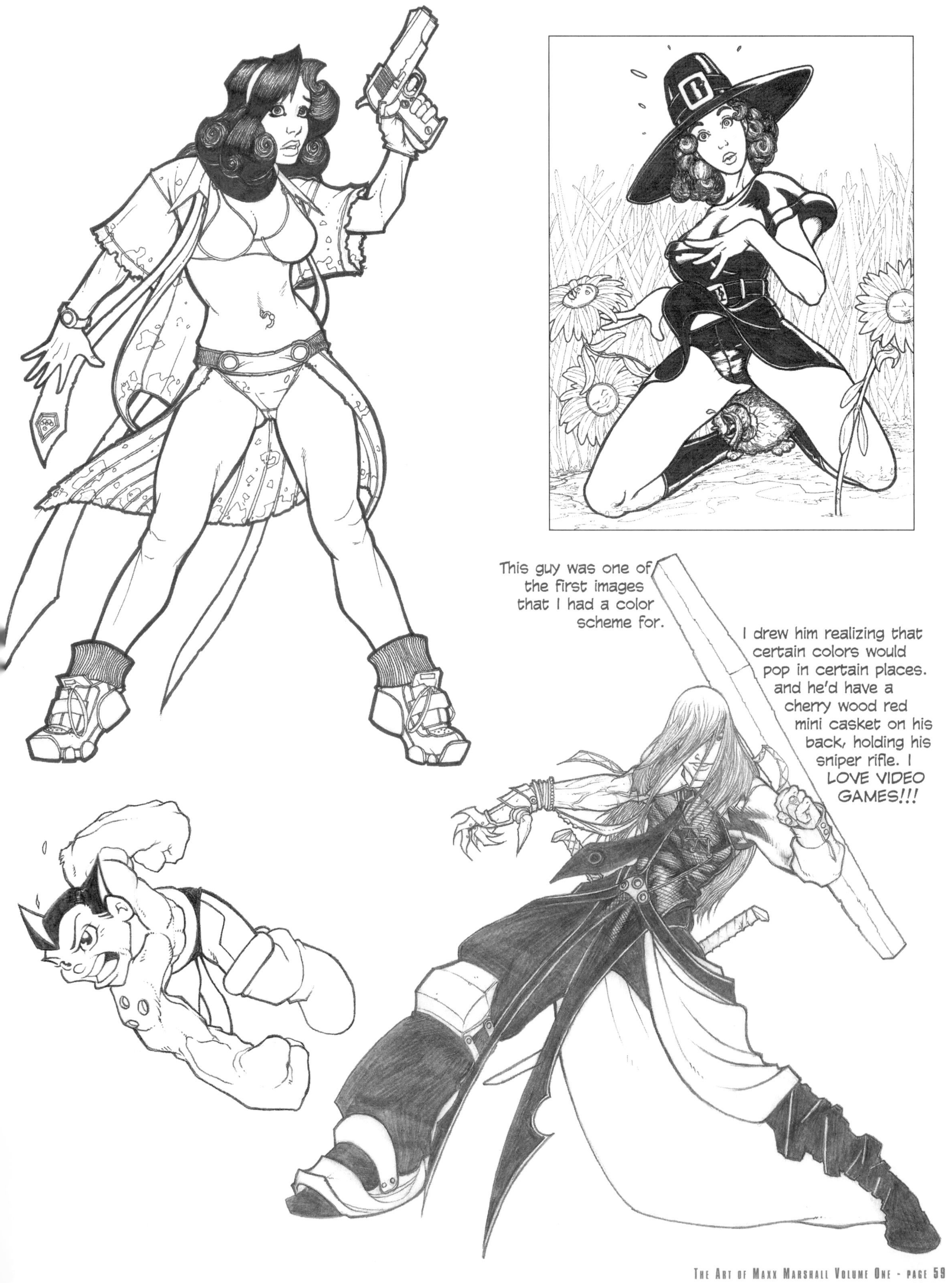
This guy was one of
the first images
that I had a color
scheme for.
I drew him realizing that
certain colors would
pop in certain places.
and he'd have a
cherry wood red
mini casket on his
back, holding his
sniper rifle. I
LOVE VIDEO
GAMES!!!

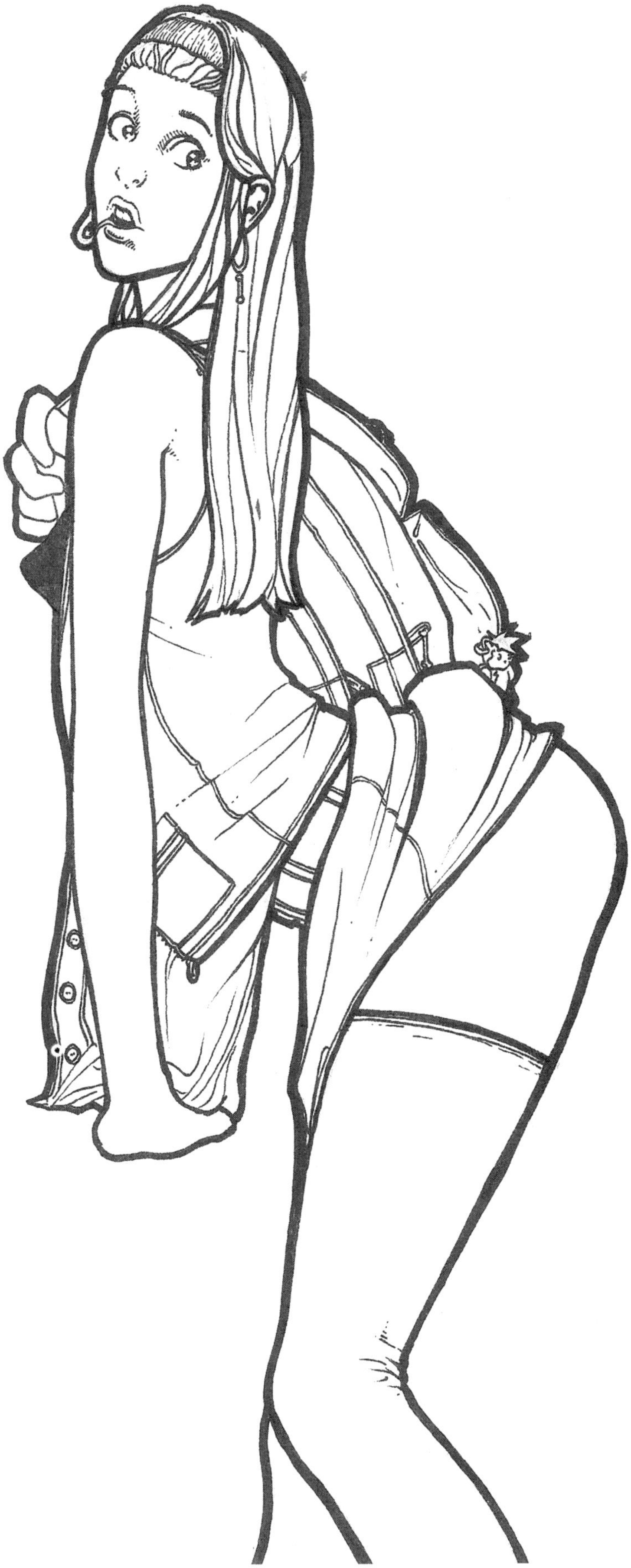

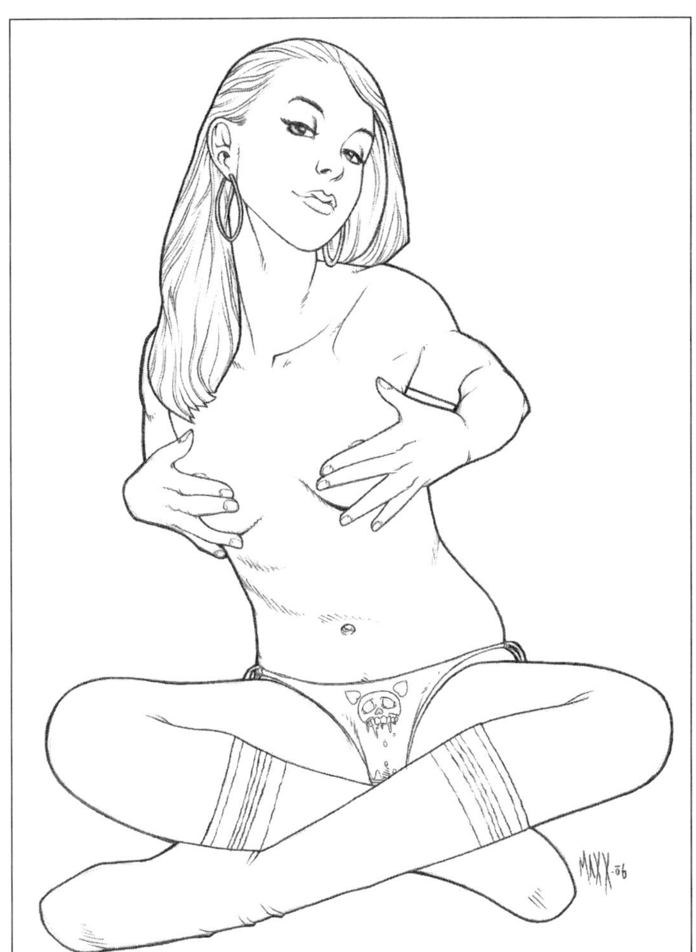
MAXX-06

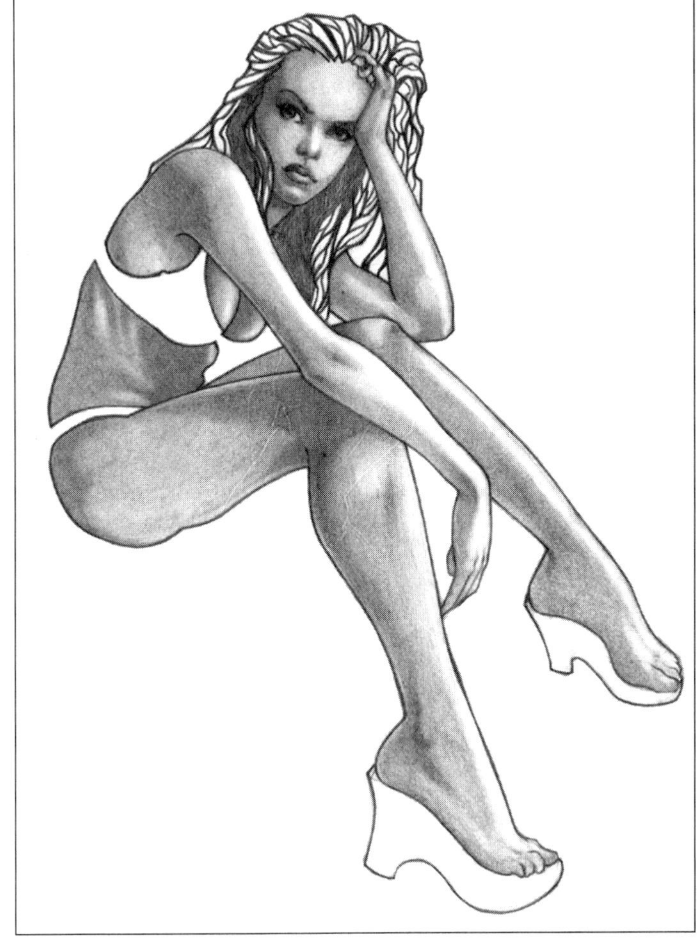

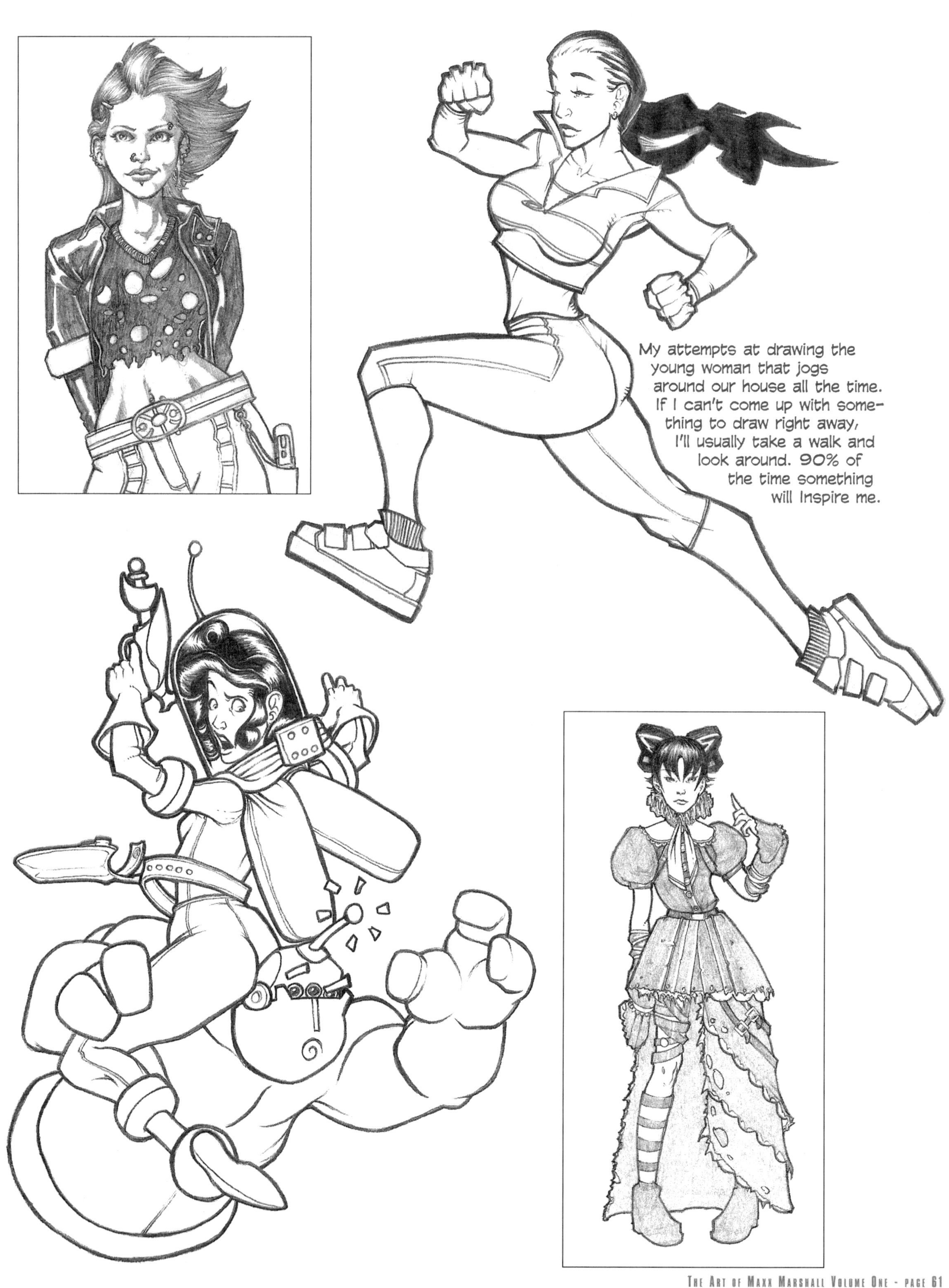
My attempts at drawing the young woman that jogs around our house all the time. If I can't come up with something to draw right away, I'll usually take a walk and look around. 90% of the time something will Inspire me.

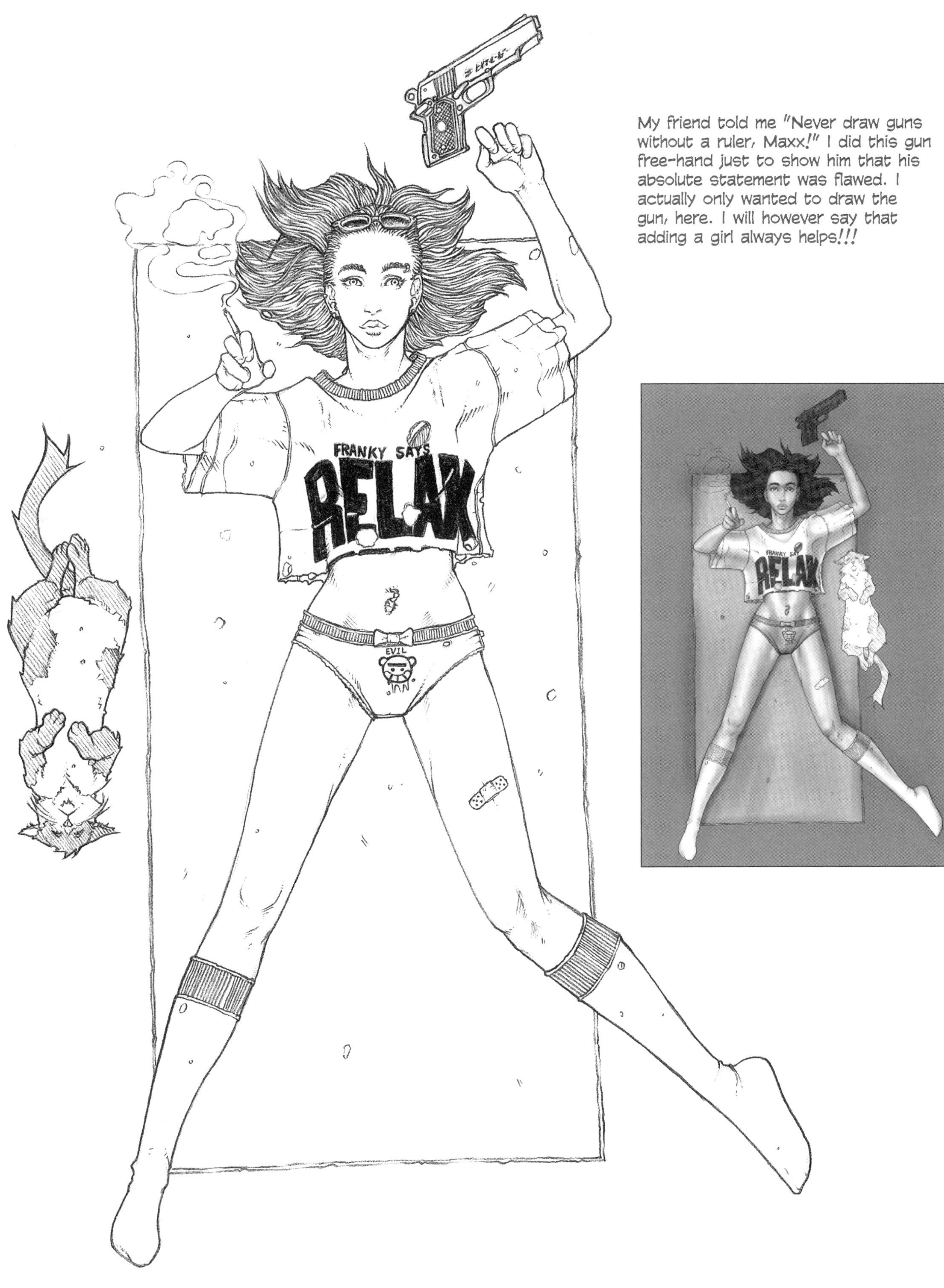

My friend told me "Never draw guns without a ruler, Maxx!" I did this gun free-hand just to show him that his absolute statement was flawed. I actually only wanted to draw the gun, here. I will however say that adding a girl always helps!!!

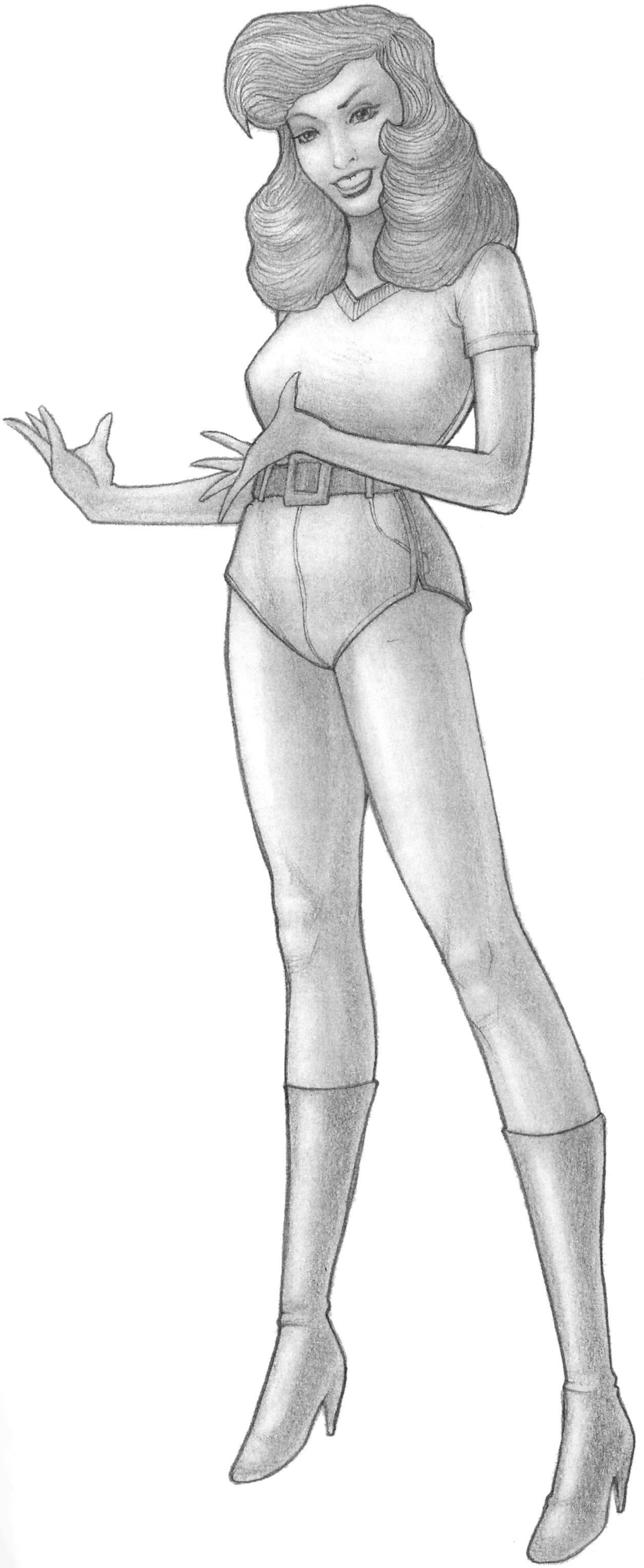

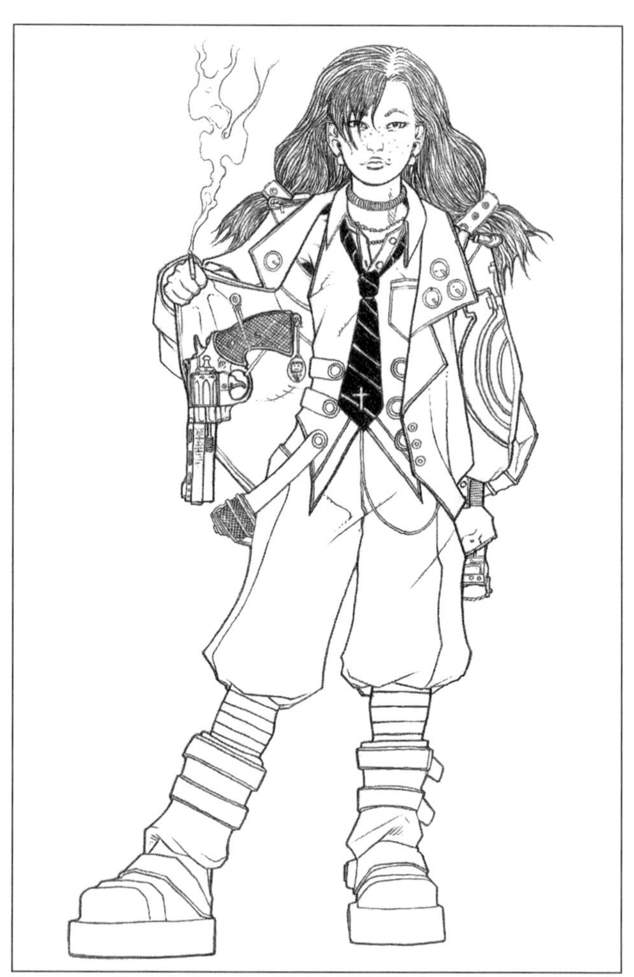

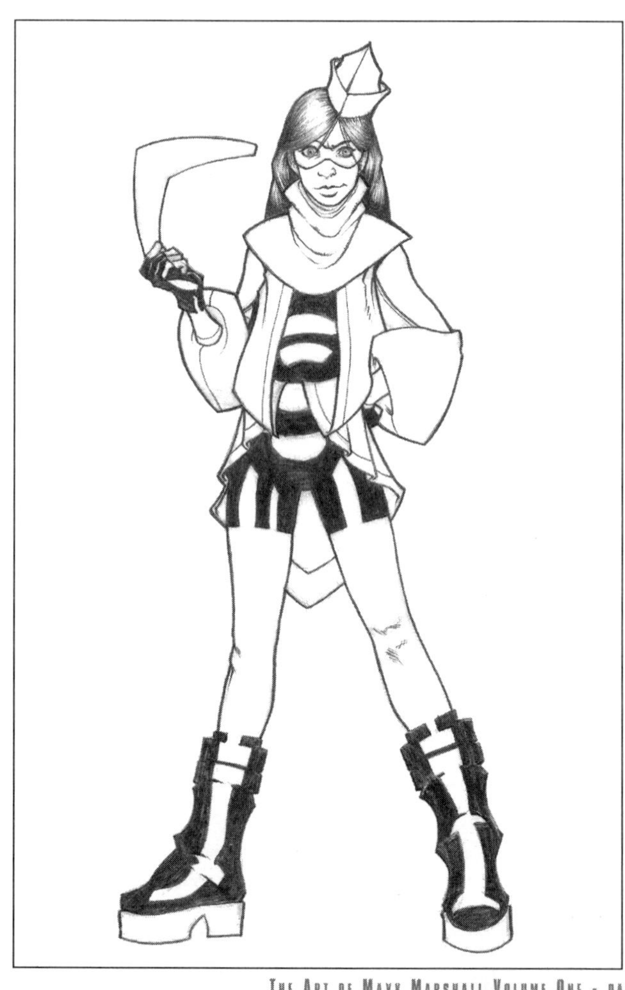

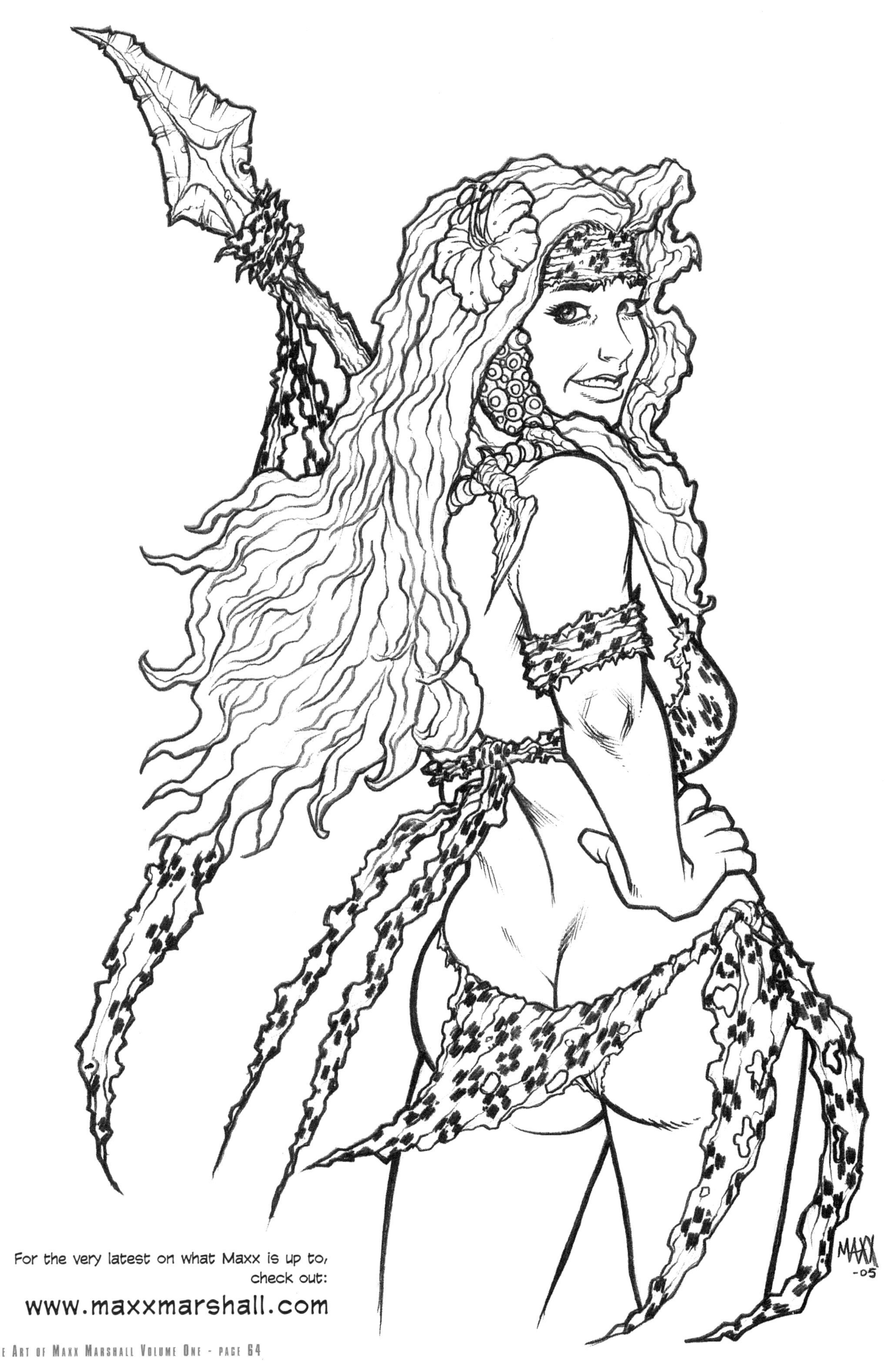

For the very latest on what Maxx is up to, check out:

www.maxxmarshall.com